Machida Karate-Do
Mixed Martial Arts Techniques

Lyoto Machida

with Glen Cordoza

Introduction by New York Times Best Selling Author
Erich Krauss

Las Vegas

First Published in 2009 by Victory Belt Publishing.

ISBN 10: 0-9815044-9-3
ISBN 13: 978-0-9815044-9-0

This book is for educational purposes. The publisher and authors of this instructional book are not responsible in any manner whatsoever for any adverse effects arising directly or indirectly as a result of the information provided in this book. If not practiced safely and with caution, martial arts can be dangerous to you and to others. It is important to consult with a professional martial arts instructor before beginning training. It is also very important to consult with a physician prior to training due to the intense and strenuous nature of the techniques in this book.

Cover Design by Michael J. Morales, VIP GEAR

Technique Photography by Brian Rule

Photograph Editing by Erich Krauss

Printed in Hong Kong

TABLE OF CONTENTS

PART ONE: STRIKING ATTACKS

1.1 : ENTERING WITH KICKS

1.2 : ENTERING WITH PUNCHES

1.3 : FOOT SWEEPS AND LEG TRIPS

PART TWO: INTERCEPTING ATTACKS

PART THREE: THE CLINCH

3.2 : ATTACKS FROM NEUTRAL CLINCH

3.3 : CLINCH DEFENSE

PART FOUR: ATTACKING THE GUARD

4.1 : ATTACKING THE DOWNED GUARD

4.2 : ATTACKING THE FULL GUARD

4.3 : ATTACKING THE HALF GUARD

PART FIVE: ATTACKS FROM DOMINANT CONTROL

5.1 : SIDE CONTROL ATTACKS

5.2 : MOUNT ATTACKS

5.3 : BACK ATTACKS

PART SIX: THE GUARD

6.1 : CLOSED AND OPEN GUARD

6.2 : BUTTERFLY AND HALF GUARD

PART SEVEN: ESCAPES

7.1 : ESCAPING CONTROLS

7.2 : SUBMISSION DEFENSE

ABOUT THIS BOOK

Before you begin studying the upcoming techniques, it is important that you understand the purpose of this manual. Although I cover dozens of striking and grappling moves, I did not include my entire martial arts system. Not only would such a task be impossible within the confines of one book, but mastering a system through text and pictures alone is very difficult. Becoming a well-rounded mixed martial artist takes a lifetime of practice, dedication, and experience. While reading and practicing the techniques in this manual will certainly help you along your journey, you should also seek out a gym or dojo with quality coaches to learn the nuances of the game, as well as train with as many martial artists as possible. In short, you need to devote yourself to your training to develop belief in yourself and the techniques you employ.

My intention with this book is to provide you with my most effective moves and strategies, most of which have been refined over several generations. Although each technique has been proven at the highest levels of competition, by no means should you operate exclusively within the borders of this book. If you already have a martial arts background, instead of casting aside what you already know, incorporate the techniques in this book into your system. If you are just starting out in the martial arts, you can use the techniques in this book as a foundation from which to build upon.

It is also important to mention that while this book focuses on mixed martial arts techniques, I'm coming out with a separate training manual that focuses exclusively on karate techniques. It will cover stance, footwork, and basic strikes in great detail. If you are interested in learning the intricacies of each of the individual strikes utilized in this book, I suggest picking up a copy of my karate book as well.

As always, I wish you the best of luck in your training.

INTRODUCTION

The Machida family.

My father, Shotokan karate master Yoshizo Machida, was a Japanese immigrant who came to Brazil in 1968 looking for adventure. Embodying the true spirit of a martial artist, he wanted to see how much he could accomplish in a country where he didn't speak the language or understand the culture.

The desire to test himself and learn his limits was nothing new to my father. Japan has a great fighting tradition, and even at the age of seven, he knew he wanted to be a part of that tradition. He began with the art of Kendo, which translates to "Way of the Sword." A mentally and physically challenging art, he learned strong martial arts values and how to wield a blade almost as tall as his body. Liking the hurdles the martial arts presented, he began training judo shortly thereafter, and when he was fifteen, he became involved in karate. By the time he arrived in Brazil, he was a third Dan in Shotokan karate and a second Dan in aikido. He had already accomplished so much in Japan, but instead of trying to bring his status with him to

Brazil, he came armed with an open mind. He found other instructors in Brazil, and through an exchange of knowledge, he continued to grow as a martial artist.

It wasn't all work for my father. In 1973 he was invited to teach karate in Salvador, a city on the northeast coast filled with easygoing people. In those days, karate was still somewhat new and mysterious, and as one would expect, he had a big social life. He was constantly being invited to various gatherings, and it was at one of these functions that he met my mother, Ana Claudia Carvalho. They dated for two years, fell in love, got married, and immediately began building a large family. They ended up having four children, all boys, and then adopting a fifth son. I was the third, and shortly after I was born, my father moved the family from Salvador to Belén do Pará, a historically rich city located on the banks of the Amazon estuary, to open his own martial arts academy.

For as long as I can remember, the entire family lived on the top floor of that academy. As one would expect form a child who is surrounded by the martial

Having fun with Karate as a youngster.

arts twenty-four hours a day, I began training at a very early age. At first it was nothing serious. I'd put on a kimono and hang around the dojo, learning the occasional defensive move. The majority of the time I was studying English or running around outside with my brothers, playing games. At the time, Belén was a wonderful place. We went adventuring down the streets and ran and climbed in the surrounding wilderness. We were always active, developing our minds and bodies. I feel very blessed for these times and freedoms because Belén is now a dangerous place, filled with so much violence. Children are forced to spend their days indoors on the computer. The city I knew growing up was different, and my brothers and I took full advantage of its luxuries.

Even though martial arts was not the center of my world at the time, I still loved to compete. I remember when I was five or six I entered the kata portion of a local karate competition. After I went out on the floor and executed my moves, I thought I had taken first place. As it turned out, I didn't even come close. My older brother Chinzo competed in the same portion of the competition, and he took second place. I remember crying my eyes out, thinking how unfair it was that Chinzo and everyone else had done better than me. In hindsight, coming in last was the best thing that could have happened to me that day. It taught me that losing was just a part of competition. All martial artists learn

that lesson at some point, but it was good that I went through it at such a young age.

In addition to the formal competitions, Chinzo and I also got into a lot of competitions at school. It would be more appropriate to call them fights, but they were never serious. They were just a child's way of releasing energy. Still, my father found himself down at the school house more often than he would have liked.

Luckily, we left those confrontations in our youth, and our father was a large part of the reason. He never forced us to train the martial arts. He wanted us to discover what we wanted, whether it be soccer, swimming, or karate. All he demanded was that we put everything into the path that we chose, to strive to be the best we possibly could. While we were making up our minds as to whether we wanted to head down the martial arts path, he taught us the importance of building our character. Every Sunday, we would gather together and listen to him tell stories about the Samurai. His stories and teachings helped pull us away from childish fights in the schoolyard and into a more respectful way of looking at the world.

As I mentioned, my training was very informal in the beginning. I'd study karate for half an hour in the afternoons, and then go out and play until evening. It wasn't until I was ten or eleven that I began to notice the effects of my training. I could feel my body getting bigger and stronger, and it was addicting. Since my father had never forced me to train, the martial arts and all it embodied was still a positive thing in my mind. Many times throughout my youth he had told me, "If the martial arts is what you want, then I will help and train you." At eleven years old, it was exactly what I wanted, and with each passing day, my desire to mas-

My brother Chinzo (right) and me.

ter new techniques became stronger.

It certainly wasn't easy. As an instructor, my father was always very rigid and hard. He demanded perfection and pushed all of his students to their limits. He didn't do so maliciously. He was from Japan, and that was their style. His goal wasn't to simply pass on martial arts techniques, but also his culture and discipline. He wanted to teach the importance of respect, what it means to have a fighter's spirit, and that a fight is just that—a fight. These lessons were hard for a lot of students to understand, but my brothers and I got it from the start. By that time, our father was already our greatest idol.

By the age of thirteen, the martial arts were in my blood. Although I trained karate with my father, I was also very curious about other styles. We hosted a weekly judo class at our dojo, and I remember watching them train, convinced that I could defeat

Competing in Sumo as a teenager.

them with my karate. Deciding to test this theory, I began playing around with them on the mat. It proved to be a tremendous amount of fun, and it also taught me a valuable lesson—there were techniques outside of karate that could benefit me as a fighter and make my karate stronger. Thirsty for all martial art knowledge, I began training with them on a weekly basis and learning a variety of clinching techniques and throws. Liking the results, I decided to continue my quest. Belén had a large Japanese colony, and every year they held a sumo event. The competition was like a giant party—in the center of the tables of food and a mingling crowd, they had a mat where sumo fighters could square off and compete. I entered this competition, and again liking what I found, I began training sumo, which not only strengthened my fighting stance and base, but also my mind.

Next came Brazilian jiu-jitsu. Although the art came from Belén do Pará, it had disappeared for a while. But when Rorion Gracie and his family created the Ultimate Fighting Championship in 1993, which proved the effectiveness of Brazilian jiu-jitsu through the victories of Royce Gracie, the art became the talk of Belén. Someone had a tape of the first event, and soon everyone had seen it. In a matter of weeks, the entire town began speaking highly about jiu-jitsu. Curiosity got the better of me, and I too checked out the tape. The instant I saw it, I knew I wanted to compete in MMA. I still wanted to be a national and world karate champion, but I was conscious of the fact that MMA would continue to grow because the sport had as few rules as possible, which was the best way to prove who was the better athlete. At fifteen, I knew I was still too young to compete in the sport, but I also knew it was waiting for me on the horizon.

Luckily, there were a few jiu-jitsu practitioners in Belén at the time, ready to cash in on the newfound popularity of the sport. Immediately I began training with Carlos Caju and Alexel Cruz, a student of the famous jiu-jitsu practitioner De La Riva. The sport continued to gain in popularity, and before long, we were offering jiu-jitsu classes in our academy.

At this point in my life, the martial arts was pretty much all I did and thought about. If I wasn't training karate with my father, I would be training with the judo boys in our academy, the sumo guys from the Japanese colony, or the jiu-jitsu practitioners in town. I knew that every martial art had its strong points, and I figured the more martial arts I trained, the more weaknesses I would eliminate from my game. And if I was interested in a martial art that couldn't be found in our area, I traveled to get the training that I needed. Later in life, I went so far as to spend forty days in Thailand, learning the art of Muay Thai, which I had very little knowledge of beforehand. However, no matter what martial arts I was interested in that week or month, my foundation always remained in the instruction I had received from my family. My goal with learning new techniques was not to replace my karate base, but rather make it stronger.

As I had expected, the UFC continued to grow in popularity, resulting in smaller promotions popping up around the world. When I was seventeen, the first MMA event came to Belén. My father knew about my obsession to compete in this type of event, and he told me that I needed to fight. Not only would it be a way to test myself, but it would also let me know for sure if I was truly interested in pursuing this type of combat.

I told the promoters of the show I wanted in, and on the day of the event, I showed up with a pair of shorts, ready to fight. Unfortunately, they decided not to let me compete. The sport was still new to them, and they didn't know how it would turn out—if someone would get seriously injured or die in the ring. Not wanting the death of a seventeen-year-old boy on their hands, they turned me away. It was frustrating, but I refused to let it stop me from getting involved in the sport.

As it turned out, it would be another eight years before I competed in my first mixed martial arts tournament. I spent that time training and teaching in the dojo, honing my skills, and competing in karate events. I remained just as dedicated as I had been throughout my teens, waking every day at 5 am for our family training session. As a result of my hard work, I won several sumo and karate tournaments, including the 2001 Pan American Karate tournament. Realizing that martial arts was not just a hobby, but rather something I wanted to build my life around, I enrolled in college and received a degree in physical education.

It's funny how things work out, because it was actually in college that I found my way into the world of MMA. I met Antonio Inoki, a famous Japanese pro wrestler and MMA promoter. Seeing potential in me, he brought me to Japan, where I trained wrestling at the New Japan Pro Wrestling dojo in Tokyo. During this time, I traveled to many places to pick up new skills. It was a very lonely time of my life, sometimes not talking to my family for a period of ten days, but I knew the isolation was a form of training in itself. Growing up, my father had taught me a valuable lesson—you are born alone, you die alone, and when you climb into the ring you are alone. Instead of letting the isolation bring me down, I used it to toughen my mind.

I made a lot of advancements in my training, and Inoki began selling me as an upcoming star in Japan. The majority of the fighters competing in MMA were grapplers or strikers from the sport of Muay Thai. I came from karate, a martial art that originated in Japan and that the public stood behind. It put a lot of weight on my shoulders. In his day, Inoki had been one of the most respected and popular athletes in the country, and I was being billed as "The Second Coming of Inoki." I was confident in my skills, but I had yet to compete in a single MMA event.

I fell back on the teachings of my father to curb my nervousness, and on May 2, 2003, I made my MMA debut in New Japan Pro Wrestling: Ultimate Crush. If I had been allowed to compete in the MMA competition in Belén when I was seventeen, I would have gotten rid of my first-fight jitters in front of a couple of hundred people. Now I would have to do it in front of 50,000 people packed into the Tokyo Dome. I had seen that many people packed into a soccer stadium before, but never for a martial arts tournament. It was nerve-racking to say the least. Overnight, I went from being a martial arts practitioner to a professional fighter.

My opponent was Kengo Watanabe, a Pancrase fighter who had taken on the likes of Bas Rutten and had competed in eighteen professional MMA bouts. My inexperience showed, because I headed into battle without a game plan on how to win. I had been training karate since shortly after I had taken my first step, yet I didn't feel comfortable employing my karate skills. For the past several years, I had been training a lot of wrestling and ground fighting, and in order to do well in the sport, I figured I had to do what all the other fighters did, which was to grab my opponent, take him to the ground, and then try to finish him with a submission.

I was able to dominate Watanabe on the mat, earning me a judges' decision after three rounds, but I was very disappointed with my victory. Minutes after the fight, I realized that I had not represented my family's style of fighting. My game was not about taking my opponent down and hitting him or going for submissions—it was about keeping the fight standing and using my karate techniques to earn the knockout. If I happened to tie up with my opponent in the clinch, that's when I should employ the wrestling and takedowns I had learned from other styles. But by forcing the fight to the ground I was ignoring the strongest aspect of my game. I promised that I would correct this mistake in my next fight, and that is exactly what I did.

Seven months after my MMA debut, I took on Stephan Bonnar, an American fighter who would later go on to be the runner-up on the first season of Spike TV's hit reality show, *The Ultimate Fighter*. Although I was still a proud member of Inoki's organization, I wanted to get some experience under my belt before my next fight in Japan, so I signed on to fight Bonnar in Jungle Fight 1, which was held in the jungle city of Manaus, Brazil.

I had my game plan down for this fight. Instead of moving into Bonnar to tie him up in the clinch, I utilized various karate movements to keep him at a distance. To acquire a dominant angle of attack, I used footwork to get to the outside of his lead leg. Once accomplished, I picked him apart with the kicks, punches, and leg trips I had been training all of my life. Before he had a chance to square his hips with mine and eliminate my dominant angle, which would allow him to hit me with an attack of his own, I disengaged and once again created distance between us. When we tied up in the clinch, instead of executing a takedown and bringing the fight to the canvas, I employed off-balancing techniques to shatter his base. Before he could reestablish his fighting stance, I followed up with more attacks.

Four and a half minutes into the first round, I had opened several cuts on his face. The fight was halted so he could be examined, and the doctor determined that he could not continue. Unlike with my first fight, I was very pleased with my performance. I felt I had properly demonstrated the effectiveness of my family's fighting style. It provided me with confidence, and I became eager to once again test my skills on the big stage over in Japan.

That confidence remained when I stepped into the ring in Kobe Wing Stadium, located in Kobe, Japan, three months later to take part in the Inoki Bom-Ba-Ye 2003 festival, but nervousness was alive in my body, as well. This was just my third fight, and I was taking on Rich Franklin, a fighter who would later claim the UFC Middleweight Championship belt. At the time, he had sixteen professional MMA fights and was widely regarded as the most dangerous fighter in the division. My trainers and manager kept telling me that he was a master striker, and that I had to be extremely careful when I fought him. They did their best to prepare me psychologically, but still I felt the pressure. In an attempt to alleviate some of that pressure, I spent a lot of time reviewing his previous fight tapes. Although my trainers were right about his skills, I believed in myself. When I looked at his tapes, I thought, "Even though he has so much experience, I can beat this guy. All he has is the luxury of starting the fight game before me."

On the night of the fight, we both came out in southpaw stances. Franklin started off the action with a rear round kick, and without thinking, I intercepted his kick with a left cross. It set a precedent for the fight. When he attacked, I'd evade his strike and counter. I had been performing such counters all of my life in the dojo, and needless to say, it was refreshing to see that they worked just as well in a real fight. My body and mind were so conditioned through repetition, I didn't even have to think. It wasn't testament to my physical prowess, but rather to the style and training methods of my family.

At one point, we got tied up in the clinch and he attempted to take me down. Due to the strong base I had garnered from practicing sumo, I was able to reverse his takedown and end up on top, in his guard. I landed some hard punches and evaded his triangle attempts, but my goal was not to dominant him on the mat. I wanted to demonstrate karate and its effectiveness, so eventually I stood up and created separation, allowing Franklin to return to his feet. As with the beginning of the fight, I bombarded him with unorthodox strikes, including back kicks and lunging punches—two techniques that you will find demonstrated later in this book. The majority of my strikes were seldom utilized in MMA competition, and they continuously caught Franklin off guard.

By the second round, I had a good feel for Franklin's rhythm. A few seconds in, he came forward with a jab, and I intercepted his punch with a cross. A moment later, he came forward with a jab/cross combination. Instead of evading both shots and then countering, I again intercepted his jab with a cross, hitting him square in the face between his punches. When you catch a fighter while he is in the middle of his combination, it will often momentarily disrupt his rhythm, which is exactly what happened here. Before he could reestablish his fighting stance and gather his senses, I tied him up in the clinch, spun him around to shatter his base, pushed him away to create separation, and then threw two strikes. The first was a knee to the face, and the second was a cross to his chin. I did not plan either strike; they both flowed naturally. They came instinctually from years of training and drilling. Landing both shots clean, Franklin dropped unconscious to the canvas.

When I first became interested in MMA at the age of seventeen, my father told me that I needed to fight to know if this was the path I wished to take. I had done that three times now, and there wasn't a doubt in my mind. Fighting was all I thought about, and when Inoki asked me if I wanted to compete against Michael McDonald, one of the most dangerous kickboxers on the planet, three months after my Franklin fight, I agreed without hesitation. A lot of fighters so new to the game might have turned down such a challenge, but no matter the outcome of the fight, I felt it could only make me stronger. There might have been better MMA fighters out there at the time, but when it came to striking, McDonald was at the top of the pile. I too was primarily a striker, and I wanted to see how my karate would fare against the skills of a champion kickboxer.

My training started off well, but there are certain inherent dangers about living in a city in the Amazon jungle. I became ill with dengue, a disease that is transmitted by mosquitoes. It is often referred to as "Bone Crusher Disease" due to the severe fever and joint pains it brings. I was as sick as I had ever been and could hardly rise out of bed, but not wanting to let my family and team down, I flew to Japan with the sickness still in my body. Although my goal was to prove the effectiveness of karate, I knew that it would not be possible in my current condition. My reactions were too slow, my body too weak. My only hope for victory would be to bring the fight to a quick conclusion, and there was only one way to accomplish that.

On fight night, I spent the first minute maintaining my distance and studying McDonald's movements. I used multiple feints to test his reactions, and when I saw a weakness in his stance, I employed a powerful lunge-step jab to close the distance and tie him up in the clinch. Immediately I established a double underhook bodylock, performed an outside trip, took him to the mat, and obtained the top half-guard position. With the goal of finishing the fight as quickly as possible, I moved back and forth between attacks. I landed strikes, worked to pass his half guard into side control, and attacked his far arm with a kimura. In an attempt to nullify my attacks, McDonald wrapped his arms around my head, and I placed my forearm into his throat. My goal was to create space so I could continue with my attack, but he didn't like the pressure. Not understanding how to escape the cross face, he simply tapped. It was not the prefect fight in terms of representing my style, but under the circumstances, I was pleased with the outcome.

The following year I had two fights. The first was against Sam Greco, which I won by split decision, and the second was against BJ "The Prodigy" Penn. BJ had already been a UFC champion, and he wanted to fight the top competition in Japan. At the time, the number one guy in the agency was Fugita, a Japanese fighter who was built like a tank. However, stepping into the ring with BJ is not a decision you make lightly. As a mundial champion, his skills on the ground were phenomenal, and he was also very proficient at striking on his feet. When Fugita turned him down, Penn challenged Sakuraba, a skilled grappler who had already defeated several members of the Gracie family, but he too turned down the fight. At the time, I was ranked number two in the organization, so they came to me next. They asked if I wanted to fight BJ Penn, and I accepted the challenge on the spot. My goal was to fight the best, and Penn certainly fell into that category.

I was in Japan at the time, so I flew back to Brazil to train. I had my work cut out for me. I knew Penn was a very complete athlete, that he could hurt you from just about anywhere, but I had always believed in myself. As long as I had the right training and discipline, I could win against anyone. Unfortunately, training didn't go as well as I had hoped. It's not that I didn't give it my all every day—it was that there simply wasn't very much time to prepare. When you factor in all the travel time from Japan to Brazil and then back to Japan, I had about twenty days of solid preparation. Personally, I like three months to get ready for a fight, but in this case that just wasn't possible.

Despite coming up from eighty-five kilos to ninety-nine kilos to fight me, Penn was still a fierce competitor. I had a distinct size advantage, but as the world learned in UFC 1, when the smaller Royce Gracie defeated much larger opponents, size isn't everything when dealing with an experienced ground fighter.

It proved to be a good back and forth battle. Penn did an excellent job setting up his takedowns with strikes, but due to my evasive maneuvers and sumo training, I managed to keep the fight standing the majority of the time and dominate him in the clinch. The one time he did manage to put me on my back, I utilized my jiu-jitsu training to prevent him from obtaining dominant positions and nullified the majority of his attacks. When I scored takedowns, I'd assume the top position, damage him with some strikes, and then return to my feet to bring the fight back into my arena. To constantly keep him guessing, I employed a lot of unorthodox techniques, such as spinning back kicks, foot sweeps, and leaping stomp kicks to the face while he was on his back. It was my toughest fight up to that point, but by employing karate footwork and offensive techniques in the clinch, I managed to implement my game plan and prevent him from implementing his, earning me a unanimous judges' decision.

That was the last time I would fight in Japan. The agency I had been working for went bankrupt, and when they closed their doors, I was left without a home. I began managing myself, but I quickly realized how difficult it was to handle both the training and business side of fighting. More than a year after my fight with BJ, I competed in another show in Brazil, which I won by TKO, but it was small-time compared to the events I had been a part of in Japan.

Not wanting to lose any more momentum, I began looking for representation. That's when I came across fight manager Ed Soares and his Black House fight team, which would eventually have a number of champions in its midst, including Antonio Nogueira, Anderson Silva, and Paulo Filho. They got me into the World Fighting Alliance—King of the Streets event, which was held in Los Angeles on June 22, 2006. Although the event wasn't televised, it boasted a lot of big names, such as Rob McCullough, Ricco Rodriguez, Jason Miller, Bas Rutten, Quinton Jackson, and Matt Lindland. As far as the fights were con-

cerned, the event was a success. Quinton Jackson won his fight with Matt Lindland by split decision, and I earned a unanimous decision over Lion's Den fighter and UFC veteran Vernon White. But despite the evening offering some technical and entertaining match-ups, the event itself didn't survive. It went bankrupt shortly after the show, but there were some positive things that came out of my involvement with it. The UFC bought several of the WFA's contracts, including those of Quinton Jackson, Heath Herring, and myself.

It was a huge opportunity for me. After fighting in Japan, my career had lost momentum. Now, overnight, I was a part of the biggest MMA organization in the world. A lot of people wondered how I would do in this new arena. In Japan, all of my fights had been in the ring, and now I would be competing in a cage. I had been told by many fighters that it was a big difference, and I had experienced that difference during my one fight in WFA. I knew I would need a lot more training to be able to use the cage to my advantage like many of the experienced UFC fighters, but personally I wasn't terribly worried. When your fighting style is based primarily on grappling, I think transitioning from the ring to the cage poses a lot of challenges because it can be used to both your advantage and disadvantage. However, I have always primarily been a stand-up fighter, and I knew that employing my karate skills would be just as easy in the cage as it had been in the ring. I felt that in the long run, I would probably like fighting in a cage more, and that's just what happened.

Sam Hodger was my first opponent in the UFC. He was a big, strong guy, but he didn't pose any danger to me during our fight. I managed to dominant him in all areas—striking, takedowns, and on the ground. Although the fight went to the judges, I saw it as a great victory because I was able to use all aspects of my game successfully. I demonstrated to the owners of the UFC and the fans that despite coming from a karate background, I was not a one-dimensional fighter.

After earning decisions over David Heath in UFC 70 and Kazuhiro Nakamura in UFC 76, I took on Rameau Sokoudjou, a fighter who had defeated both Rogerio Nogueira and Ricardo Arona in the Pride Fighting Championships in Japan. Rogerio was a good friend of mine, and a very dangerous fighter. When Sokoudjou knocked him out, it made an impact. The UFC had brought him aboard for these impressive victories, but many of the fighters in the UFC wanted nothing to do with Sokoudjou. He was one of those guys who seemed to get stronger by the day.

Despite Sokoudjou's size and prowess as a fighter, I agreed to the challenge. I knew that he was very dedicated to his training, but I also knew that it would be very difficult for him to get to me due to my leg kicks and karate techniques. And if he somehow did manage to bring me to the ground, which is where he had caused a lot of damage in his previous fights, I felt I could use my ground skills to defend his attacks and turn the fight in my favor.

The few days leading up to the fight proved to be extremely stressful. My passport approval had been delayed in Brazil, and it didn't arrive until one day before the fight. In addition to this, everyone around me kept talking about how dangerous a fighter Sokoudjou was. The combination of these stresses added up, and I had to meditate for long hours in order to get into a focused frame of mind.

Luckily, the fight went exactly as I had expected. Sokoudjou was fast and explosive, but I prevented him from taking me to the ground using my evasive techniques. Starting to get frustrated, he hesitated for a moment in the fight, and that is when I struck him and knocked him down. Instead of giving him time to recover, I went down with him, wore him out with ground and pound, transitioned to side control, and then submitted him with a kata-gatame choke, a technique you will find demonstrated later in this book.

It turned out to be an important fight for me because all bets had been on Sokoudjou. People said that he was too fast and too strong. I had won several fights in the UFC at that point, but all had been by decision. People didn't yet fully understand my elusive fighting style, but when I beat Sokoudjou, I began to gain a little popularity. However, it was nothing compared to the popularity I gained in my next fight, which was against the Huntington Beach Bad Boy, Tito Ortiz.

The months leading up to the fight proved difficult for me due to the feud going on between UFC president Dana White and Tito. They hated each other to all ends, and I somehow got caught in the middle. Tito kept saying that he wanted to get me because it would be the same thing as beating up Dana White. And Dana kept saying that I would beat Tito without a doubt. I tried to make it clear to both sides that the controversy belonged to them, that I wanted nothing to do with it, but I kept ending up in the middle. I just wanted to show up and do my job.

Despite this pressure, the fight went well. I was able to dominate Tito from beginning to end, in all three arenas. I managed to implement my game plan without letting him implement his, which was to put me on my back, press my head up against the cage, and then beat me up. He did manage to catch me in a good triangle choke toward the end of the match, but my will to escape was bigger than his will to win. There was no way I was going to tap—I wanted to win at all cost. After dominating him for three rounds, I earned the unanimous decision.

Overnight, my popularity in the United States grew, which is something I really needed. I'd had some battles with big, strong fighters, yet my name was not known. Beating a fighter as popular as Tito gave value to my career. However, there was still a lot of criticism floating around, people saying that I was a boring fighter because most of my battles went to decision. But that was my style, using footwork to evade my opponent's attacks and wear him out. And then, when he was frustrated and making mistakes, I moved in for a rapid attack. It had proved very effective up to that point, but I also realized that fighting was a business. In addition to being a good fighter, you also had to entertain the fans.

There was no way I was going to redesign an effective fighting style that had taken a lifetime to build, but there were certainly improvements I could make. The primary one came in the form of going in for the kill when I had my opponent injured. It could prove risky because many fighters recover quickly, which would put me directly in the danger zone, but I was part of a fighting family, and I had to do what would make that family happy.

I gave the fans a show in my next fight. I took on dangerous striker Thiago Silva, and after wearing him down for the entire first round, I landed a hard punch that knocked him to the canvas. Instead of maintaining my distance and continuing with my evasive style, I jumped on top of him and battered him with strikes, earning the TKO.

The win made me the top contender in the division, and on May 23, 2009, I stepped into the Octagon to fight Rashad Evans for the UFC Light Heavyweight title belt. I used the exact same strategy I had with

Silva. Evade Evans's attacks, and then counter with attacks of my own. When the implementation of my game plan had him visibly frustrated, I went in for the kill. I hit him with a barrage of strikes, knocking him out cold. A few seconds later, I had the UFC Light Heavyweight title belt wrapped around my waist.

It was the greatest moment of my life because it proved to the world the effectiveness of my family's fighting style. Since the first UFC, karate had been viewed as an ineffective martial art. But there is a difference between karate competition and karate as a martial art. To make karate competitions more popular and mainstream, they had outlawed the more dangerous strikes. As the years progressed, karate practitioners began to distort karate and train in the wrong way. The essence of karate was lost.

My family never bothered with this type of karate. We had spent decades training and adapting karate-do, the karate that existed before competition. None of the techniques we practiced were for point sparring. All of them were designed for full-contact fighting. On top of this, we trained correctly. My father had taught me at an early age that fighting was less about putting time in at the gym and more about training properly. Every strike and drill we performed had a purpose.

We trained karate in its full form, which embodied not just the technical aspect of the sport, but also the philosophical aspect. We learned the culture of the martial arts, which made discipline and determination our priority. We learned that if you really wanted to achieve your goals, you had to make sacrifices. And if those goals are strong enough in your mind, those sacrifices will be a pleasure.

Since my early teens, I had been on a constant quest to better myself every day. I had always tried to find new challenges to incorporate into my training. I knew I was not the best fighter, but I also knew that if I followed the path of karate, I could one day reach the top of the mountain, not just in fighting, but also in life. The karate my family studied was responsible for the man I had become, and by winning the UFC belt, I felt I had done the art form justice.

For all of my family, karate gave us our foundation. Everything we have achieved and all the lessons we have learned, both inside and outside the ring, we owe to our father and the style of karate he brought over from Japan. For my brothers and me, karate is in our blood. My oldest brother, Take, is a third Dan

and one of the best people I know. He teaches at the academy and works on the administrative side as well. My older brother Chinzo was the vice champion in the Japan Karate Association World Championships in 2006, which was held in Sydney, Australia. He is always by my side, helping me train. My younger brother, Kenzo, is also a dedicated martial artist, and he took the training he received out into the world and used it to become a famous reporter here in Brazil. Even our adopted brother, Francisco, has followed our family tradition. He received a degree in physical education, and he puts that knowledge to use in the academy.

For all of us, the philosophical side of karate has always been more important than the technique because it has prepared us for life. It's taught us how to handle relationships, understand hardship, and let things roll off our backs. When I stop fighting, I would like to pass along all the knowledge I have gained from my family. I want to show this path to everyone, not just athletes. Karate provides a life foundation, one that teaches people to be better, honest, and to respect others. Once you have this foundation, you can be whatever you want—a journalist, a lawyer, a doctor. Everyone can use the culture and philosophy of karate. It teaches you to learn from everyone, from a little child to an elderly person. It teaches you to pay attention and see.

My brothers and I with our father.

PART ONE
STRIKING ATTACKS

When you move toward your opponent and launch an attack, the goal is to land powerful strikes without compromising your position or making yourself vulnerable to counterattacks. Although there are hundreds of different combinations that can be utilized to achieve this goal, in this section I have included the ones that have worked best for me. As you will see, the majority of my attacks begin with a fake strike, which is often referred to as a feint. The goal of the feint is not to hurt my opponent, but rather to distract him and cause a certain reaction.

Another key component of my fighting style is to utilize the high-low or low-high principle of attack. For example, I will throw a fake low kick to pull my opponent's focus to the lower half of his body and cause him to drop his hands, creating a perfect opportunity to follow up with a punch directed at his exposed face. Along these same lines, I will throw a punch at my opponent's face to pull his focus high and cause him to elevate his guard, leaving the lower half of his body vulnerable. Although the majority of combinations in this section are based upon this principle, it is important not to get locked into any one method of attack. While it is possible to figure out how the majority of opponents will react to your initial strike, and then base your follow-up strikes upon the openings created by that reaction, not everyone fights the same. If your opponent has studied your style and trained to keep his guard high when you throw low kicks, following up with a punch to his face might not be your best option. For this reason, it is important to stay flexible in the ring and build combinations on the spot based upon the openings available.

Acquiring a dominant angle of attack is another component to executing successful combinations. Anytime you move toward your opponent with a combination of strikes, you are vulnerable to counterattacks. To limit that vulnerability, you want to move to the outside of his centerline. However, this is often difficult to achieve. If you simply step to the outside of your opponent's body to acquire a dominant angle, chances are he will immediately square his hips with your hips to eliminate your dominant angle. As a result, it often takes some trickery. One method is to utilize a feint strike to distract your opponent. While he is focused on defending your fake strike, you move off to his side to acquire a dominant angle and then launch an attack before he can square his hips with yours.

It is also possible to acquire a dominant angle after executing your combination. For example, if you and your opponent both have your left foot forward, and you execute the left inside low kick to left jab combination (p. 24), you want to immediately circle toward your left upon completing your combo. This not only removes your body from your opponent's line of fire, but it also puts you in an excellent position to follow up with another combination. As you will see, in this section I have included numerous combinations that utilize these two methods.

Stance is another component that plays an important role in the combinations I demonstrate. Some combinations are best utilized when squared off with your opponent in the same stance, meaning you both have the same foot forward, while others are more effective when you are squared off in the opposite stance, meaning you have opposite feet forward. To help guide you in the right direction, I've broken up the sections in this part of the book into two categories. One focuses on same-stance combinations, while the other focuses on opposite-stance combinations. Sometimes a combo will involve reversing the positioning of your feet to execute a specific strike, while other times you remain in your original stance throughout the duration of the technique. By varying your attack in this manner, you remain unpredictable and make it difficult for your opponent to launch an effective counter.

Like stance, distance also dictates the strikes that you can utilize in your combinations. When you launch your initial attack, your opponent has three primary options. He can come forward and attack, hold his ground, or retreat. The option he chooses will decide what type of follow-up strike you can throw, whether it be a kick, punch, elbow, or knee. For example, if you enter with a punch and your opponent backs away into kicking range, you have a couple of options. You can immediately follow up with a kick or close off the distance by stepping forward, which allows you to throw a punch, elbow, or knee. To help you better understand how distance plays a role in your combinations, I've broken this part of the book into three sections—entering with kicks, entering with punches, and foot sweeps and leg trips. Although I offer specific combinations based upon an opponent's most common reaction to the initial strike in the combo, it is important to remember that all opponents act differently. If the second strike in the combo calls for a kick but your opponent holds his ground after the initial strike, you must be able to adapt to the situation and employ the best strike for the job. The only way to become a master at making these types of split-second decisions is to spend countless hours sparring and drilling in the gym.

1-1: Entering with Kicks

In this section I demonstrate multiple combinations that utilize a kick as the initial strike. There are several benefits to this—it allows you to initiate your attack from outside of punching range, and it often pulls your opponent's focus down to the lower half of his body, allowing you to follow up with a secondary strike to his face. When studying the techniques, it is important to pay special attention to the dynamics of the initial kick. Oftentimes, it is strictly a feint and should be thrown with just enough power to capture your opponent's attention. A perfect example is when you use

a low round kick to the inside of your opponent's lead leg to set up a cross to his face. In this case, throwing a hard kick would most likely disrupt your base, making it very difficult to flow directly into the cross. While it is certainly possible to throw a hard low kick, reset your base, and then fire off the cross, it increases your opponent's ability to block your power shot, as well as counter with strikes of his own. However, there are certain combinations where throwing the initial kick with power will serve you best. I recommend learning both types of combinations because the best way to get the upper hand in a fight is to keep your opponent guessing. If every combination you throw begins with a feint kick, your opponent will catch on and begin focusing on defending against your secondary attack instead. But if half of your combos begin with devastating kicks, your opponent will have no choice but to respect your initial strikes, allowing you to pull him into your traps again and again.

1-2: Entering with Punches

In this section I demonstrate numerous combinations that utilize a punch as your initial attack. Again, the goal of this initial strike is not always to cause your opponent damage. In most cases, it is designed to distract your opponent from your secondary strike. However, in order for this type of feint to work, you must throw your punch into his line of vision. This serves two purposes. First, it allows you to momentarily blind him, which makes it difficult for him to see your secondary strike approaching. Second, it allows you to grab one of his hands and pull it downward as you draw your punching arm back into your stance. Not only does this shatter his guard and create a pathway for your secondary strike, but it also makes it very difficult for him to launch a counterattack. But just as when you initiate your attack with a kick, it is important to constantly switch things up. As you will see in this section, some of the combinations involve landing the initial punch with the intent to cause damage, and others are simply thrown as a distraction. By switching back and forth between these two types of combos, your opponent will have no choice but to treat each of your punches as a dangerous blow, producing the reactions you need to land your secondary strike.

1-3: Foot Sweeps and Leg Trips

When you move forward and attack, whether it is with a feint or an actual strike, chances are your opponent will react. A lot of times that reaction will create an opening to execute a sweep, either by kicking his legs out from underneath him or using his positioning to trip him to the mat. In this section, I demonstrate how to set up and execute the sweeps that have worked best for me in mixed martial arts competition. Although all of these techniques are in the form of an attack, it is important to note that they will also work anytime your opponent is off balance, which happens quite often when you evade one of his strikes.

Once you have mastered the basic flow of movements, start getting creative. Anytime your sparring partner shifts his weight to strike or defend, try knocking his leg or legs out from underneath him using one of the techniques in this section. Even when he doesn't collapse to the mat, he will often be thrown off balance, which creates a perfect opportunity for you to flow directly into an attack.

One of the best parts about these techniques is that they work against all fighters, regardless of their martial arts background. They are just as effective against a championship kickboxer as they are against a world-class wrestler. Another nice attribute about these sweeps is that they keep you on your feet, which gives you the option of remaining standing or following your opponent to the mat. This is an excellent choice to have in MMA competition. If you feel your ground game is better than that of your opponent, you can drop down on top of him and secure top control. If you want to keep the fight standing, you can hover over him and land strikes to his legs and face before the referee stands him back up. However, it is also important to react to the situation. If you manage to stun your opponent with a strike and then sweep him to the mat, even if your goal is to keep the fight standing, it can be beneficial to follow him to the mat and attempt to finish him off. Remaining standing in such a scenario gives your opponent time to recover, and this is not a mistake you want to make. When I fought Sokoudjou in the UFC, I hit him with a powerful cross and then tripped him to the mat. Although he was very skilled on the ground and under normal circumstances it was in my best interest to keep the fight on the feet, I followed him down and capitalized on his stunned state by finishing him with a kata-gatame choke, which you will find demonstrated in the tail end of this book.

TOOLS TO HELP DEVELOP YOUR STRIKING COMBINATIONS

Drills

To develop the timing, sense of distance, coordination, speed, and power needed to launch effective combinations, you must drill them relentlessly in the gym. There are many ways to drill. If you have a training partner, you can practice them on the focus mitts, Thai pads, and while sparring. If you don't have a partner, you can practice them on the heavy bag or while shadow boxing. For the best results, you want to do all of the above. If you neglect the drilling aspect of training, it will be extremely difficult to develop the fluidity needed to catch your opponent off guard and land your strikes clean.

Heavy Bag

All of the combinations demonstrated in this section can be performed on a heavy bag. It's a quintessential tool because you can throw your strikes at full power without the mental stress of getting hit, which in turn allows you to focus on developing your technique. For the best results, you want to use a Muay Thai heavy bag that reaches all the way to the ground. This lets you direct your strikes both low and high. It is important to mention that while doing heavy bag work will do wonders to develop your speed and power, it will do little to develop your timing. To build this much-needed attribute, it is very important to include partner drills into your training regimen.

Shadow Boxing

Shadow boxing is another drill you can do without a partner. Although it does little to develop your power, it will help develop your speed and coordination. To get the most out of this drill, it is important not to get lazy with your movements. Picture an imaginary opponent standing in front of you, and then move around him as you throw your strikes. The nice part about shadow boxing is that it will prepare you for when you miss a strike in a fight. The more you shadow box, the easier it will be to regain your balance off a failed punch or kick and flow directly into your next technique.

Pads

Having a partner hold pads for you while you fire off combinations is one of the best ways to develop the attributes necessary for pulling off the techniques; it develops speed, power, coordination, timing, and distance. You can have your partner shout out the combination or free spar. Either way, this is an aspect of training that should not be overlooked.

Sparring

There is no substitute for the real thing. Once you feel comfortable executing the techniques on pads, it is time to start sparring. If you neglect this aspect in training then you will never develop the reactions or confidence necessary for executing an effective attack. However, sometimes it can be difficult to practice new techniques in a live sparring situation. To help you develop your technique, have your opponent defend while you come forward with your attack. Once accomplished, switch directions and have him attack while you defend. Take turns going back and forth, one guy firing off the combination while the other reacts and presents the target. The goal is not to hit your opponent but to get used to the reactions that the combinations produce. This will not only do wonders to develop your timing, but it will also give you confidence in your technique. Once you feel comfortable, start free sparring.

LEAD INSIDE LEG KICK TO RIGHT CROSS

This combination begins with a kick to the inside of your opponent's lead leg, but the goal is not to cause your opponent damage with the strike. Its primary purpose is to pull his focus down to his legs, creating an opening to land a cross to his face. For a smooth transition, do not draw your leg back into your stance after landing the kick. Instead, drop your foot straight down to the mat. This puts you in range to land the cross, as well as allows you to use the downward step to generate more power in the punch. Like most of the combinations that I demonstrate, all of the movements should be performed fluidly with no lag time between strikes.

Chinzo and I are in standard stances with our left foot forward. Both of us are searching for an opening to attack.

Shifting my weight onto my right leg, I rotate my hips slightly in a clockwise direction, pivot my right foot so that my toes are pointing toward my right side, and lift my left foot off the mat.

I throw a left leg kick to the inside of Chinzo's lead thigh. It's important to note that instead of throwing this kick hard, I just tap my foot lightly on his leg. This draws his attention downward, creating an opening for the follow up cross.

4

With Chinzo's focus now on his legs, I step my left foot straight down to the mat and prepare to launch a right cross toward his face.

5

As I drop my left foot, I drive off the mat with my right foot, rotate my hips and shoulders in a counterclockwise direction, and throw a right cross toward Chinzo's face. As my arm extends, I turn my palm toward the mat and keep my left hand elevated to protect myself from counterstrikes.

6

Still rotating my hips and shoulders in a counterclockwise direction, I land a powerful right cross to Chinzo's chin. Having turned my hand over, I make contact with only the knuckles of my index and middle fingers. It's important to notice the positioning of my body as I land the strike. I've kept my posture straight, my hips in line with my shoulders, and my left hand up to protect the left side of my face. To protect the right side of my face, I've shrugged my right shoulder.

LEAD INSIDE LEG KICK TO JAB

This combination is very similar to the previous one in that you start your attack by throwing a kick to the inside of your opponent's lead leg. The goal of the kick is the same—to distract your opponent and draw his focus down to his legs, creating an opening to throw a secondary strike at his face. However, instead of throwing a cross as your secondary strike, you throw a jab. While the jab doesn't pack nearly as much power as the cross, it is a quicker strike. To ensure you cause damage, step your kicking leg into your opponent's comfort zone immediately after landing the kick. This allows you to use the forward momentum of your body to generate additional power in your punch. If you look at the photos below, you'll notice that as I land the jab, I angle my body away from my opponent's centerline. This is critical because it removes your body and head from his line of fire, making it difficult for him to counter. It also provides you with a dominant angle of attack that will allow you to follow up your combination with more strikes.

I'm squared off with Chinzo in my fighting stance. Both of us are looking for an opening to attack.

I throw a left kick to the inside of Chinzo's lead thigh. Instead of putting all my power into the kick, I simply tap his leg to draw his attention toward the lower half of his body and distract him from the punch that will immediately follow.

Driving off the mat with my right foot, I drop my left foot toward the outside of Chinzo's right leg.

Still driving off the mat with my right foot to propel my body forward, I plant my left foot on the mat to the outside of Chinzo's right leg and throw a left jab toward his face.

As I plant my left foot on the mat, I rotate my fist in a clockwise direction so that my palm is facing the ground and land a jab to Chinzo's chin. It's important to mention that unlike the kick in this combination, the jab is meant to be a power shot. In order to land the hardest blow possible, I've harnessed the forward momentum of my body. To protect my face from counterstrikes, I've kept my chin tucked to my chest, my right hand up, and shrugged my left shoulder above my chin.

As I draw my left hand back toward my body, I pivot on my left foot and slide my foot across the mat in a clockwise direction.

Having angled my body to the outside of Chinzo's line of fire, he must square his hips with mine before he can launch an effective counterstrike. To capitalize on his awkward positioning, I reestablish my fighting stance and prepare to immediately employ another attack.

LEAD FRONT KICK TO JAB

This combination begins with a front kick to your opponent's sternum, which is an excellent strike to use against fighters who constantly move forward. Unlike in the previous two combinations, this initial kick doesn't lower your opponent's focus down to his legs due to the height of your target, but it is still an excellent way to set up a strike to the face. When you land the front kick hard enough, you force your opponent to hunch forward and his guard to momentarily drop, making his face vulnerable to attack. To capitalize on that vulnerability, drop your kicking leg straight down to the mat instead of pulling it back into your stance. This allows you to use the downward momentum of your leg to generate power for the jab. Unless you knock your opponent out with this second strike, there is a good chance that he will attempt to immediately counter, so it is important to angle your body away from his line of fire as you throw the punch.

I'm squared off with Chinzo in my fighting stance. Both of us are searching for an opening to attack.

Shifting my weight onto my right leg, I lean back slightly and lift my left leg straight up off the mat.

3

Having elevated my left knee, I drive the ball of my left foot into my opponent's abdomen.

4

After I land with the front kick, I propel my body forward by driving off the mat with my right foot. At the same time, I coil my left leg into my body. This last step is very important. If you drop your left foot to the mat immediately after landing the kick, you will most likely fall forward, compromising your balance and decreasing the power of your punch.

5

Having re-chambered my leg, I step my left foot to the mat and land a stiff left jab to Chinzo's chin. Notice how I use the forward momentum of my body to generate power for the strike. From here I will circle to the outside of his body to secure a dominant angle and set up more strikes.

REAR FRONT KICK TO LUNGE-STEP JAB

In this sequence I demonstrate how to use a powerful rear front kick to your opponent's midsection to set up a lunge-step jab. Just as with the previous technique, the goal of the kick is to double your opponent over and cause his hands to drop, making his face vulnerable to attack. However, in order to shatter your opponent's guard in this fashion you must throw a proper kick. First, do not rotate your shoulders as you throw the kick because it telegraphs your movements and makes it easier for your opponent to avoid your attack. Second, elevate the heel of your kicking leg up to your buttocks before driving the ball of your foot into your target. This allows you to generate the maximum amount of speed and power in your kick. Third, draw your heel back into your buttocks to re-chamber your leg before stepping your foot to the mat. This will reset your base and give you control over your forward momentum. Lastly, do not pull your leg back into your stance after landing the kick. Instead, drop your foot straight down and plant it to the outside of your opponent's lead leg, reversing your stance. This lets you harness the forward momentum of your body in your punch. Although the regular jab isn't nearly as powerful as the cross, the lunge-step jab possesses more power than any other punch. Landing a clean strike will often lead to a knockout, but just in case your opponent has an iron jaw, it is important to pivot away from his centerline as you land your strike. In addition to making it difficult for him to launch a counterstrike, it also provides you with a dominant angle of attack and allows you to immediately follow up with another combination.

I'm squared off with Chinzo in my fighting stance. Both of us are looking for an opening to attack.

Shifting my weight onto my lead leg, I coil my right heel to my right buttock and prepare to throw a rear front kick to Chinzo's midsection. When executing this movement, it is crucial that you keep your shoulders squared up with your opponent. If you turn your body even slightly, you will telegraph the kick and your opponent will most likely defend against it.

I lift my right knee toward my chest.

Having elevated my right knee to my chest, I extend my leg and drive the ball of my right foot into Chinzo's abdomen.

5

Keeping my knee elevated, I coil my right heel back toward my right buttock.

6

Instead of pulling my right leg back to reestablish my fighting stance, I drive off the mat with my left foot and step my right foot toward the outside of Chinzo's lead leg.

7

Still driving off the mat with my left foot, I plant my right foot on the mat and land a powerful right jab to Chinzo's jaw. In order to execute this technique properly, you want to land the punch just as your lead foot touches the ground. If you throw the punch after your foot touches down, your forward momentum will be lost and the punch will lack power.

8

Having landed clean with the right jab, I shift my weight onto my right leg, rotate my body in a counterclockwise direction, and slide my left foot across the mat.

9

I continue with my previous actions.

10

Having secured a dominant angle of attack, I assume my fighting stance and start plotting my next attack.

REAR FRONT KICK TO HIGH ROUND KICK

Like the previous combination, this one begins with a rear front kick to your opponent's midsection. As you know, landing a clean shot will usually cause his body to hunch forward and his guard to drop, making his face vulnerable to attack. While the lunge-step jab is an excellent way to capitalize on that vulnerability, it is important to constantly switch up your attacks to keep your opponent guessing. In this combo, you change the lunge-step jab to a high round kick to his head. As with most striking combinations, it is important not to pause between strikes. The instant you land the front kick, drop your foot to the outside of your opponent's lead leg and then launch the round kick with your opposite leg.

I'm squared off with Chinzo in my fighting stance. Both of us are searching for an opening to attack.

Shifting my weight onto my lead leg, I coil my right heel to my right buttock and prepare to throw a rear front kick to Chinzo's midsection. It's important to remember to keep your shoulders locked in your stance when you throw the front kick. Turning your shoulders telegraphs your kick and gives your opponent a chance to defend against it.

I lift my right knee toward my chest.

Having elevated my right knee to my chest, I extend my leg and drive the ball of my right foot into Chinzo's abdomen.

Keeping my knee elevated, I coil my right heel back into my right buttock.

I step my right foot to the mat, switching my stance. It's important to notice the positioning of my right foot. My toes are pointed toward my right side and my foot is positioned to the outside of my opponent's lead leg. The former opens my hips, which will allow me to throw a fast and more powerful kick, and the latter positions my body out of my opponent's line of fire should he throw a counterstrike.

Keeping my left leg coiled, I elevate my left knee, pull my right shoulder back, and twist my hips in a clockwise direction.

Continuing to pull my right shoulder back and twist my hips in a clockwise direction, I pivot on my right foot so my heel is facing my opponent. At the same time, I throw my right arm behind me to generate power for the kick and maintain balance, extend my left leg, and drive my shin into the side of Chinzo's head.

SIDE STEP TO SIDE KICK TO CROSS

As you may have noticed, I concluded many of the previous combinations by circling to the outside of my opponent's body to acquire a dominant angle of attack, which in turn sets me up to launch a secondary combination. In this sequence, I circle to the outside of my opponent's body before launching my combination. This can sometimes be difficult to accomplish because without distracting your opponent with strikes, he will often spot your movement and counter with movement of his own. To avoid such an outcome, I begin the combination by rotating my hips and shoulders, just as I would when throwing a rear roundhouse kick. While my opponent is distracted by this movement, I step my lead foot to the outside of his rear leg, acquiring a dominant angle of attack. Before he realizes that my initial round kick is just a fake, I elevate my rear leg and deliver a side kick to his sternum.

Technical Note: If you look at the photos below you'll notice that I pull my knee into my chest and re-chamber my leg before stepping my foot to the mat. This is a crucial step because it allows you to reset your base before following up with the cross. If you drop your foot to the mat immediately after landing the kick, the momentum from the kick will carry you forward, compromising your balance and decreasing the power of the cross.

Chinzo and I are in standard stances with our left foot forward. Both of us are looking for an opening to attack.

I take a lateral step with my lead leg, positioning my foot to the outside of Chinzo's body, and turn my shoulders in a counterclockwise direction. By moving my body in this manner, I not only position myself to throw a powerful side kick, but I also trick my opponent into thinking that I'm throwing a rear round kick.

Shifting my weight onto my left leg, I lean back slightly to maintain balance and lift my right knee toward my chest.

With my right knee elevated, I thrust my hips forward and drive the heel of my foot into Chinzo's abdomen.

Before I can lower my right foot to the mat and follow up with another strike, I first have to reset my base. I accomplish this by pulling my knee into my body and coiling my right foot toward my right buttock.

With my balance intact, I step my right foot to the mat and prepare to launch a left cross at Chinzo's face.

Shifting my weight onto my right leg and driving off the mat with my left foot, I pull my right shoulder back and rotate my hips in a clockwise direction.

Continuing with my previous actions, I come up onto the ball of my left foot and throw a left cross to the right side of Chinzo's jaw.

INSIDE LEG KICK TO SPINNING BACK KICK

This is a very crafty combination. It begins by throwing a lead round kick to the inside of your opponent's lead thigh, but instead of pulling your leg back into your stance after landing the kick, you continue with your rotation and plant your foot to the outside of his lead leg. It is important to mention that the goal of the initial kick is not to cause your opponent damage, but rather to distract him. If you throw the kick too hard, your leg will rebound off his thigh, making it difficult for you to continue with your rotation. To ensure success, simply tap his leg with your foot and then use your circular momentum to step your foot over his leg and to the mat. If you look at the photos in the sequence below, you'll notice that this turns my back to my opponent and sets me up to deliver a powerful spinning back kick to his midsection. The key to success with this combo is making a quick transition between kicks. As you can see in the photos, my opponent attempts to counter my initial kick with a right cross, which is quite common. By being quick to transition into the spinning back kick, I land my second strike before he can land his cross. If you hesitate while your back is turned for even a fraction of a second, you will be vulnerable to a slew of counterstrikes.

1 Chinzo and I are in standard stances with our left foot forward. Both of us are searching for an opening to attack.

2 Shifting my weight onto my right leg, I rotate my hips slightly in a clockwise direction, pivot my right foot so that my toes are pointing toward my right side, and lift my left foot off the mat.

3

I throw a left kick at the inside of Chinzo's lead thigh. If you look at the photo closely, you'll notice that I simply tap my foot against his leg. This pulls his focus down to the lower half of his body, creating an opening for the spinning back kick.

4

Keeping my eyes locked on my target, I rotate my body in a clockwise direction and plant my foot to the mat. It's important to notice the positioning of my left foot. My heel is pointing toward my opponent and my leg is positioned to the outside of his lead leg. This primes my hips to throw the back kick and positions my body to the outside of his centerline. In an attempt to capitalize on my positioning, Chinzo launches a right cross toward my face.

5

Using the momentum of my turn to my advantage, I lean my upper body forward and throw a back kick into Chinzo's abdomen. By leaning forward, I not only put my head out of punching range, but I also counterbalance my weight.

REAR LOW ROUND KICK TO LUNGE-STEP CROSS TO HOOK TO REAR ROUND KICK

This is a more complex combination that follows the high-low and low-high theme of attack. To begin, you throw a rear round kick to the outside of your opponent's lead leg. While in most combinations you would pull your leg back into your stance after landing the kick, in this combo you immediately lower your foot after impact and plant it to the outside of your opponent's lead leg. In addition to switching your stance, this action also gives you a dominant angle of attack, allowing you to transition seamlessly into a cross. Once you land your second strike, there is a good chance your opponent will attempt to counter. To continue your assault safely, you throw a lead hook and circle your rear leg farther to the outside of your opponent's body at the same time, removing yourself from his line of fire. When your hook lands clean, the majority of the time it will turn your opponent's back to you even more. As you can see in the sequence below, this presents an excellent opportunity to conclude your combo with another hard round kick to your opponent's lead leg. Although I personally like this combination, it is important to experiment as much as possible to find what works best for you. As long as you keep with the high-low and low-high principle, move to the outside of your opponent's body to acquire a dominant angle of attack, and don't hesitate between your strikes, you will have no problem landing clean shots time and again.

Chinzo and I are in standard stances with our left foot forward. Both of us are looking for an opening to attack.

Shifting my weight onto my lead leg, I rotate my hips and shoulders in a counterclockwise direction, come up onto the ball of my rear foot, and prepare to throw a right low round kick to Chinzo's lead thigh.

Pulling my left shoulder back and rotating my hips in a counterclockwise direction, I fire a right round low kick to Chinzo's left leg. It is important to note that you don't want to throw this kick with the intent to cause damage. By throwing it lightly, you pull your opponent's focus downward, yet still have the balance needed to immediately transition to the left cross.

Instead of retracting my right leg and reestablishing my original stance, I drive off the mat with my left foot and plant my right foot on the mat to the outside of Chinzo's lead leg.

Still driving off the mat with my left foot, I shift my weight onto my right leg, come up onto the ball of my left foot, rotate my hips and shoulders in a clockwise direction, and land a left cross to Chinzo's chin. To protect the right side of my face from counterstrikes, I keep my right hand up at chin level.

As I retract my left arm, I pull my left shoulder back, rotate my hips in a counterclockwise direction, and throw a right lead hook to the left side of Chinzo's face.

As my punch sails toward Chinzo's face, I continue to rotate my hips in counterclockwise direction and begin sliding my left foot circularly across the mat. It is important to note that this rotation not only provides your punch with more power, but it also gives you a dominant angle of attack.

As I plant my left foot on the mat, I land a powerful right hook to Chinzo's face. It's important to notice that my right fist, elbow, and shoulder have all travelled circularly along the same horizontal plane. To protect the right side of my jaw, I have shrugged my right shoulder. To protect the left side of my face, I have kept my left hand up at eye level.

With Chinzo stunned from the right hook, I pull my right shoulder back, pivot my right foot so that my toes are pointing to my right, rotate my hips in a clockwise direction, and prepare to unleash a left round kick to the front of Chinzo's lead leg.

Still pulling my right shoulder back and rotating my hips in a clockwise direction, I extend my left arm and launch a left round house kick to Chinzo's lead thigh.

Continuing with my previous actions, I dig my left shin into the front of Chinzo's left leg.

SWEEPING KICK TO CROSS TO FLYING KNEE

This is another combination in which you use a low kick to set up a powerful strike to your opponent's face. While a low round kick is best utilized when in kicking range, the sweeping kick in this combo is best utilized when in punching range. The difference with this strike is that instead of crashing your shin against the inside of your opponent's thigh, you sweep your foot into his calf muscle. The goal is not to cause your opponent damage with the strike, but rather momentarily spread his legs apart and cause him to drop his hands in an attempt to correct his balance. The instant he lowers his guard, you follow up with a cross to his unprotected face. Sometimes the punch will knock your opponent down, and other times it will knock him backward. If the latter is the case, an excellent option is to conclude the combination with a flying knee to the midsection or face. However, it is important to note that when you execute a flying knee both of your feet momentarily leave the ground, making it impossible to defend against your opponent's counterstrikes. To avoid getting hit while in midair, throw your knee toward your opponent's centerline but move your body off to his side.

Chinzo and I are in standard stances with our left foot forward. Both of us are looking for an opening to attack. Notice how we are currently in punching range.

I throw a sweeping kick to the inside of Chinzo's lead leg. It is important to mention that this technique should only be employed when you are squared off with your opponent in punching range. If you are in kicking range, employing a low round kick to the inside of his thigh is a better option.

Having disrupted Chinzo's balance and drawn his attention downward with the foot sweep, I drop my left foot to the mat and prepare to throw a right cross at his face.

Driving off my right foot, I shift my weight onto my left leg, pull my left shoulder back, come up onto the ball of my right foot, and throw a right cross to the left side of Chinzo's jaw.

5

As I pull my right arm back into my stance, I hook my right hand around Chinzo's lead hand, breaking his guard and creating an opening for the left jumping knee.

6

To capitalize on Chinzo's positioning and stunned state, I elevate my right knee to my chest, leap upward by driving off the mat using my left foot, and reach my left hand to the left side of his head.

7

As I leap forward into the air, I scissor my legs and hook my left hand around the back of Chinzo's head.

8

Pulling down on Chinzo's head with my left hand, I thrust my hips forward and drive my left knee into his body.

REAR MID-RANGE ROUND KICK TO CROSS

This is a highly effective kick-punch combination that can be utilized when you and your opponent are in opposite fighting stances. To begin, throw a rear round kick to your opponent's liver. Although striking with the ball of your foot can be very effective, in this particular case you want to strike with your shin because it brings you closer to your opponent, which allows you to immediately follow up with a cross. If you look at the photos below, you'll notice that I do not land the kick, pull my leg back into my stance, and then throw the cross. Instead, I throw the cross as I pull my kicking leg back toward my stance. This allows you to use the backward momentum of your leg to generate power for the punch. It's not the easiest technique to master, but it is a very dangerous combination once you get the hang of it.

Chinzo is in a standard stance with his left leg forward and I am in a southpaw stance with my right leg forward. Both of us are looking for an opening to attack.

Before Chinzo can get his offense going with a strike, I pivot my right foot so that my toes are pointing to my right, extend my right hand to the outside of his left hand, rotate my hips in a clockwise direction, and launch a left round kick toward his mid-section.

As I drive my left shin into Chinzo's midsection, I cup my right hand over the top of his left wrist.

Having disrupted Chinzo's focus, I curl my left heel to my left buttock, lean my upper body slightly forward, and chamber my left hand in preparation to throw a left cross. Notice how I use my right hand to pull down on my opponent's left hand. This prevents him from defending against my attack, as well as hinders him from throwing a counterstrike.

Still controlling Chinzo's left wrist with my right hand, I kick my left leg back and land a left cross to his chin. It's important that you land the cross as you pull your kicking leg back. If you reset your base before throwing the cross, your opponent will see the punch coming and most likely defend against it.

Rotating my body in a counterclockwise direction, I draw my left arm toward my body, pull my left leg back, and return to my fighting stance.

I reestablish my fighting stance and begin plotting my next attack.

REAR MID-RANGE ROUND KICK TO SPINNING BACKFIST

When you and your opponent are in opposite fighting stances, throwing a mid-range round kick is an excellent way to set up a spinning backfist. To make a fluid transition between strikes, do not pull your kicking leg back into your stance after landing your kick. Instead, continue with your rotation and plant your kicking leg to the outside of your opponent's lead leg. This not only removes your body from your opponent's line of fire, but it also allows you to flow directly into the spinning backfist. The key to being successful with this combination is using the initial rotation of your kick to deliver the backfist. If you make the combination two separate movements, you become vulnerable to a number of counterattacks.

Chinzo has assumed a standard stance and I've assumed a southpaw stance. Both of us are searching for openings to attack.

I begin my attack by stepping my lead foot toward my right side and positioning my foot to the outside of Chinzo's left leg. As I do this, I turn my body in a clockwise direction and reach my left hand toward his left arm. It's important to notice how the toes of my right foot are pointing toward my right side. This primes my hips to throw a fast and powerful round kick.

Still rotating my body in a clockwise direction, I shift my weight onto my right leg, latch on to Chinzo's left wrist with my left hand, and launch a left round kick toward his abdomen. It is important to mention that grabbing my opponent's hand not only prevents him from blocking the strike, but it also prevents him from throwing a counterattack.

I land a left roundhouse kick to Chinzo's abdomen.

Instead of pulling my left leg back into my stance, I follow through with the kick and circle my left leg around the outside of Chinzo's lead leg. At the same time, I release my left grip on his left hand.

6

Still rotating my body in clockwise direction, I plant my left foot to the outside of Chinzo's lead leg.

7

I pull my right shoulder back while continuing to rotate my hips in a clockwise direction. As I do this, I shift my weight onto my left leg, turn my head so that I can get an eye on my target, and throw a right backfist toward Chinzo's face.

8

Using the momentum of my turn to generate power, I throw my right fist into the side of Chinzo's face. Notice how I land the strike with the side of my fist. Assuming this positioning prevents me from injuring my hand and causes significant damage to my opponent.

LOW HOOK KICK TO CROSS

The low hook kick to cross is another striking combination that is best employed when you and your opponent are squared off in opposite stances. The low hook kick is not a long strike, so unless you begin in punching distance, you must step your rear foot forward to get into range. Once you have closed the gap, circle your lead leg to the inside of your opponent's lead leg and drive your heel into his thigh. When done properly, you not only cause damage to your opponent's leg, but you also knock him off balance, creating a perfect opening to deliver a cross to his face. The nice part about this combination is that the hook kick is highly unorthodox in MMA competition and often catches your opponent off guard.

Chinzo has assumed a standard stance and I've assumed a southpaw stance. Both of us are searching for openings to attack.

In order to land clean with the low hook kick, I first have to close the distance. I accomplish this by stepping my left foot forward and planting it next to my right foot. It's important to notice how I am pointing the toes of my left foot toward my left side. This primes my hips to throw a fast low hook kick with my right leg. It is also important to notice how I lean my upper body slightly back to maintain my balance as I execute the kick.

Transferring my weight onto my left leg, I elevate my right knee toward my left side.

Leaning my upper body slightly back, I straighten my right leg and flex my foot so that my heel is in line with Chinzo's lead thigh.

5

Using the hamstring muscle of my right leg to curl my right foot inward, I dig my right heel into the inside of Chinzo's left thigh.

6

I curl my right heel into my right buttock to re-chamber my leg.

7

Driving off the mat with my left foot, I step my right foot to the outside of Chinzo's left leg and prepare to throw a left cross at his face.

8

Shifting my weight onto my right leg, I pull my right shoulder back, rotate my hips in a clockwise direction, come up onto the ball of my left foot, and deliver a left cross to Chinzo's chin. To guard the left side of my face from counterstrikes, I've shrugged my left shoulder into my chin. To protect the right side of my face, I've kept my right hand elevated.

SIDE STEP TO LOW ROUND KICK TO HIGH ROUND KICK

This is another combination that is best employed when you and your opponent are in opposite fighting stances. Unlike in the previous combination, you do not attack your opponent head on. Instead, you start by stepping to the outside of his body to acquire a dominant angle of attack and remove yourself from his line of fire. Once positioned off to his side, you throw a lead round kick to the outside of his thigh. The goal with this initial kick is not to cause your opponent damage, but rather draw his focus downward. The instant his attention drops, you throw a rear roundhouse kick to his head. To be effective with this combo, it is very important that both kicks are thrown back to back. If you lag between your strikes, your opponent will most likely adjust to your positioning and defend against your attack.

Chinzo has assumed a standard stance and I've assumed a southpaw stance. Both of us are searching for openings to attack.

Driving my left foot off the mat, I step my right leg forward and toward my right side.

3

I slide my left foot to my right foot. Notice how the toes of my left foot are pointed toward my left side. This action primes my hips to throw a fast right leg kick to Chinzo's lead thigh.

4

Shifting my weight onto my left leg, I lean my upper body slightly back, rotate my hips in a counterclockwise direction, and throw a right low kick to Chinzo's left hamstring.

5

Instead of pulling my kicking leg back to its original position, I switch my stance by dropping my right foot straight down to the mat.

I transfer my weight onto my right leg, pull my right shoulder back, and start rotating my hips in a clockwise direction.

Still pulling my right shoulder back and rotating my hips in a clockwise direction, I throw a left round kick toward Chinzo's head.

As I whip my hips around, I throw my left arm back to generate power for the kick and counterbalance my weight.

LOW ROUND KICK TO HIGH ROUND KICK

This combination is similar to the previous one in that you throw a lead round kick to your opponent's thigh and then follow up with a rear round kick to his head. The primary difference is timing. Instead of landing your first kick, pulling your leg back into your stance, and then launching your second kick, you throw both strikes almost simultaneously. When you throw two strikes almost on top of each other, it shatters your opponent's defensive rhythm. However, the technique is not risk free. Anytime both of your feet leave the mat, you become vulnerable to your opponent's counters. To lower your risk with this combination, I recommend employing it in the later rounds of a fight when your opponent's reactions have slowed.

Chinzo has assumed a standard stance and I've assumed a southpaw stance. Both of us are searching for openings to attack.

To begin my attack, I step my lead foot slightly forward and toward my right, pull my left shoulder back, and start rotating my hips in a counterclockwise direction.

I slide my left leg forward and throw a right round kick to the outside of Chinzo's lead thigh. It's important to note that when I throw the kick, I DON'T rotate my hips and throw my leg along a circular path as I normally would. Instead, I keep my hips somewhat square and throw my leg at an upward angle so that my foot just glances my opponent's leg. Remember, your goal is to draw your opponent's attention downward so you can set up the high kick, NOT to cause damage. It's also important to note how I throw my lead arm back. This is not to generate power for the kick. I do this to counterbalance my weight so that I can immediately switch the rotation of my hips and throw the rear roundhouse kick.

I elevate my right knee toward my chest and shoot my body upward by driving off the mat using my left foot. At the same time, I pull my right shoulder back, throw my right arm behind me, and swing my left arm up and toward my right side.

Having elevated my body off the mat, I drop my right leg toward the mat, throw my left arm back to generate power and counter-balance my weight, whip my hips in a clock-wise direction, and swing my left leg along a circular path toward Chinzo's face.

Fluid with my movements, I land a hard flying round kick to right side of Chinzo's head.

Technical Note: When first starting out, it can be difficult to launch a rear round kick while your lead leg is still in the air. To develop your coordination, practice the combination on a heavy bag in the form of a drill. To begin, throw a kick to one side of the bag and then as you retract your leg, drive off your opposite foot to propel your body into the air and kick with your other leg, striking the opposite side of the bag. Ideally, you want to perform this drill on a Muay Thai heavy bag that reaches the floor. This allows you to throw your kicks low or high. The goal is to string together as many kicks as you can without touching both feet to the ground. At first you may only get two kicks off before you lose your balance and have to reestablish your stance. But with enough practice, you will be able to throw several kicks in a row, stringing them together into an endless combination. You can go for a set amount of reps or do it in time increments. When done correctly, this drill will not only develop your coordination, but it will also build speed, power, and cardio, as well as strengthen your core and legs.

HOOK KICK TO CROSS TO STRAIGHT KNEE

After you've successfully landed a couple of hard rear round kicks and rear front kicks to your opponent's body, the chances are he will expect the strikes and defend against them. To keep your opponent guessing, it's important that you mix it up. In the sequence below, you start your combination by throwing a rear hook kick to the side of your opponent's head. As you land with the kick, bring your kicking foot back into your fighting stance and then immediately step forward and land with a straight cross. When you land the cross, it is likely that your opponent will retreat backward. To make up the distance, it's important that you step your rear leg forward and switch your stance. Once accomplished, grab the back of his head, break his posture, and fire a knee to his midsection. Like the previous technique, this is another combination that is best utilized in the later rounds of the fight when your opponent's reactions have slowed due to fatigue. This increases your chances of landing clean with your first strike and reduces the chances of him defending against your second and third strike.

Chinzo has assumed a standard stance and I've assumed a southpaw stance. Both of us are searching for openings to attack.

I step my right foot forward and plant it to the outside of Chinzo's left foot. As I do this, I pull my right shoulder back and reach my left arm across my body.

Still pulling my right shoulder back, I rotate my hips in a clockwise direction, shift my weight onto my right leg, and elevate my left foot off the mat by curling my left heel toward my left buttock. At the same time, I latch on to Chinzo's left wrist with my left hand. With this control, I not only prevent him from blocking the hook kick, but I also hinder him from throwing a counterstrike.

4

As I turn my hips in a clockwise direction, I lift my left knee toward my chest. To break Chinzo's guard and create an opening to land with the hook kick, I pull his left arm down using my left hand. Notice that my left leg is positioned to the outside of his lead leg.

5

Having elevated my knee to my chest and created an opening for the hook kick with my previous actions, I lean my upper body back, swing my left leg in an arcing motion, and dig my left heel into the side of Chinzo's neck.

6

Leaning forward to counterbalance my weight, I drop my right foot toward the mat.

7

I rotate my hips in a counterclockwise direction and pull my left leg back. It's important to notice how I am still controlling Chinzo's left arm with my left hand.

ENTERING WITH KICKS

I plant my left foot on the mat and momentarily assume a southpaw stance. At the same time, I release my left grip on Chinzo's left wrist and wrap my right hand over the top of his left hand. This keeps his guard broken, preventing him from firing a counterstrike or defending against my next attack.

Driving off the mat with my left foot, I shift my weight onto my right leg, pull my right shoulder back, and rotate my hips in a clockwise direction. To break Chinzo's guard and create an opening to attack, I sweep his left arm downward and toward my right side using my right hand.

Continuing with my previous actions, I come up onto the ball of my rear foot and throw a left cross at Chinzo's chin.

As I land the left cross, Chinzo begins to fall backward. To capitalize, I allow the momentum from the cross to carry my weight forward.

As Chinzo retreats straight back, I step my left leg forward, switching my stance, and wrap both of my hands around the back of his head.

Having broken the distance between us with a forward step, I shift my weight onto my left leg, pull Chinzo's head down using both of my arms, and fire a right knee toward his abdomen.

Still controlling Chinzo's head with my left hand, I pull my right shoulder back to generate power for the strike, curl my right heel toward my right buttock, point my toes toward the mat, and drive my right knee into his solar plexus.

CROSS TO LUNGE-STEP OVERHAND

In this sequence I demonstrate how to set up a lunge punch using a right cross. If you look at the photos below, you'll notice that I do not throw the cross with the intentions of hitting my opponent. Instead, I throw it from outside of punching range to distract and momentarily blind him, creating an opportunity for me to step my rear leg forward and throw a stealthy overhand at his face. When studying the technique, it is important to notice that I do not switch my stance and then throw the overhand, but rather throw the overhand as I reverse my stance. This allows me to harness my forward momentum in the punch, producing a knockout blow. If you pause between punches, your overhand will not only be less powerful, but your opponent will most likely see it coming and defend against it. It is also important to notice that as my opponent elevates his arms to defend against my initial cross, I grab his lead hand and drive it downward. This breaks his guard and creates a pathway for me to land clean with the overhand.

Chinzo and I are in standard stances with our left foot forward. Both of us are looking for an opening to attack.

I come up onto the ball of my right foot, drive forward, pull my left shoulder back, rotate my hips in a counterclockwise direction, and throw a right cross toward Chinzo's face to distract and momentarily blind him.

Still driving forward off my right foot, I shift a larger portion of my weight onto my left leg and start pulling my right hand back toward my body.

As I draw my right arm back into my body, I hook my right hand over the top of Chinzo's left hand and break his guard. At the same time, I step my right leg forward to switch my stance.

Having broken Chinzo's guard with my previous actions, I plant my right foot on the mat, shift my weight onto my right leg, and come up onto the ball of my left foot. As I do this, I pull my right shoulder back, rotate my hips in a clockwise direction, and land a left overhand to Chinzo's face. When you move your right leg forward, it is important to position your foot to the outside of your opponent's lead leg. This is a crucial step for several reasons: It puts you in range to land with the overhand; the momentum of the forward step generates additional power in the punch; and it removes your body from your opponent's line of fire should he throw a counterstrike.

CROSS TO HIGH ROUND KICK

In this sequence I demonstrate how to use a cross to set up a round kick to your opponent's head. Just as with the previous combination, I use the cross to momentarily blind my opponent. This allows me to grab hold of his lead arm, break his guard by forcing his arm downward, and then launch a round kick at his head. It is important to note that in order to be successful with this type of trickery, you must execute both strikes as one fluid movement. If you delay between the punch and the kick, your opponent will most likely employ defensive movements or a counterstrike.

Chinzo and I are in standard stances with our left foot forward. Both of us are searching for an opening to attack.

Before Chinzo can get his offense going, I pull my left shoulder back, rotate my hips in a counterclockwise direction, and throw a right cross toward his face.

Having momentarily blinded Chinzo with my right cross, I pull my right hand back into my stance and reach my left hand toward my right side. To cover the distance needed to land with the left round kick, I slide my rear foot forward. As I plant my right foot to the mat, I shift my weight onto my right leg and lift my left foot off the mat. It's important to note that I position my foot so that my toes are pointing toward my right. This allows me to fluidly transition from the slide step to the kick, as well as adds power to my strike.

Still pulling my right shoulder back, I grab Chinzo's left wrist with my left hand, rotate my hips in a clockwise direction, and throw a left round kick toward his face.

To break Chinzo's guard and further distract him from the approaching kick, I pull on his left hand with my left hand. With his guard broken, I lean my upper body slightly back and land a left round kick to the right side of his face.

CROSS TO HOOK TO HIGH ROUND KICK

When you are fighting an elite striker, you often have to use multiple feints to create one opening to attack. In the sequence below I demonstrate how to use a cross and a hook to set up a high roundhouse kick. Just as with the previous combo, the cross doesn't need to be thrown at full power. Its main goal is to distract and momentarily blind your opponent. However, it is important to make contact with the hook. In addition to disrupting your opponent's balance, it will drive his head directly into your round kick, producing a devastating final blow.

Chinzo and I are in standard stances with our left foot forward. Both of us are searching for an opening to attack.

I step my left foot forward and to the outside of Chinzo's right foot. At the same time, I throw a right cross toward his face, but my intention is not to land with the strike. My primary goal is to distract him from the left hook that will immediately follow.

As I draw my right hand back into my stance, I rotate my body in a clockwise direction and throw a left hook toward the right side of Chinzo's face.

Using the momentum of my clockwise turn, I pivot on my left foot, slide my right foot circularly across the mat, and land with a left hook.

Having drawn Chinzo's focus away from my legs, I pull my left arm back into my body, shift my weight onto my left leg, rotate my hips in a counterclockwise direction, and lift my right leg off the mat.

6

Leaning my upper body slightly back, I extend my right arm to counterbalance my weight and throw a right round kick toward Chinzo's face.

7

Continuing with my previous movements, I land a powerful right round kick to the left side of Chinzo's face.

JAB TO CROSS TO SPINNING HOOK KICK

A lot of times when you advance toward your opponent with two straight punches, such as a jab and a cross, he will either retreat in a straight line or lean his head backward. Although a lot of times his defensive movement will allow him to evade your initial strikes, it puts him just outside of punching range with his weight distributed on his heels, making him vulnerable to the spinning hook kick. If you look at the last photo in the sequence below, you'll notice that I connect with the bottom of my foot to avoid injuring my training partner. However, it is important to note that you always want to strike with your heel in a fight. If you fail to do so, you will cause little to no damage with the strike.

Chinzo and I are in standard stances with our left foot forward. Both of us are searching for an opening to attack.

Driving off the mat with my right foot, I slide my left foot forward and throw a left jab toward Chinzo's face to distract and momentarily blind him.

As I draw my left hand back toward my body, I rotate my hips slightly in a counterclockwise direction and throw a right cross toward Chinzo's face. Again, my goal is not to land the strike, but rather distract my opponent and force him to shift his weight back onto his heels.

As I extend my right arm, I reverse the rotation my hips to generate momentum for the spinning hook kick.

To add momentum to my clockwise turn, I pull my right arm toward my body and turn my head toward my right.

6

Still twisting my body in a clockwise direction, I bend my left knee slightly while pivoting on the ball of my left foot.

7

With my wound-up hips and shoulders tugging on my right leg, I release that tension by shifting all of my weight onto my left leg.

8

Using the momentum of my clockwise turn to throw the kick, I drive the bottom of my right foot into the right side of Chinzo's face. To counterbalance my weight, I drop my left shoulder toward the mat and extend my right arm. It is important to note that I struck my brother with the bottom of my foot to prevent from injuring him. If you are in a fight, you want to flex your foot and strike with your heel.

FAKE KICK TO COUNTER CROSS

Attacking your opponent with a barrage of telegraphed strikes is a risky endeavor, especially when up against a good counterstriker. A much better approach is to begin with a feint and then employ a combination based upon your opponent's reaction to that feint. In the sequence below, I step my lead foot to the outside of my opponent's rear leg, just as I would when preparing to throw a rear round kick. With my opponent being a good counterstriker, he spots my movement and immediately steps forward with a jab aimed at my face. His goal is to land his linear strike before I can land my circular strike. Having produced a reaction out of my opponent, I immediately reverse my direction and shift my body to the outside of his lead leg. This not only causes him to miss with his strike, but it also gives me a dominant angle of attack. Before he can pull his outstretched arm back into his stance, I capitalize on his vulnerability by throwing a powerful cross at his face. The most important part of this combination is quickly shifting from one side of your opponent's body to the other. If you move toward his right side and then lag before shifting to his left, he will be able to hone in on your head or body and land with his strike.

Chinzo and I are in standard stances with our left foot forward. Both of us are searching for an opening to attack.

To fake the rear round kick, I step my left foot to the outside of my opponent's body and slide my right foot across the mat. Anticipating the kick, Chinzo steps his left foot forward and throws a jab.

As Chinzo extends his left arm, I drive off the mat with my left foot and lunge toward my right. This footwork not only causes my opponent to miss his jab, but it also makes him vulnerable to my cross.

Having removed my body from Chinzo's line of fire, I come up onto the ball of my rear foot, shift my weight onto my left leg, pull my left shoulder back, rotate my hips in a counterclockwise direction, and throw a right cross toward his face.

Continuing with my previous movements, I land a powerful right cross to the left side of Chinzo's face.

CROSS TO OUTSIDE LEG SWEEP

In order to land clean with a strike you must first penetrate through your opponent's guard. In the previous sequence I demonstrated how to accomplish this using a feint, and in this sequence I demonstrate how to accomplish this using a hand trap when in opposite fighting stances. It's a rather simple technique. As I step forward and throw a cross, I hook my lead hand around my opponent's lead hand and force it downward. In addition to clearing a pathway for my cross, it also makes it very difficult for my opponent to launch an effective counter. It is important to note that unlike in several of the previous combinations, the cross should be thrown with power to force your opponent's weight off of his lead leg. This allows you to immediately follow the cross with an outside leg sweep. To accomplish this, do not pull your arm back into your stance after landing the punch. Instead, wrap your punching arm around the front of your opponent's body and use it to push him backward. As you force his weight further onto his rear leg, hook your lead leg around the outside of his lead leg and sweep it out from underneath him. When timed correctly, your opponent will collapse to his back, creating numerous opportunities to attack.

1

Chinzo has assumed a standard stance and I've assumed a southpaw stance. Both of us are searching for openings to attack.

2

Driving off the mat using my left foot, I lunge my right foot forward. As I close the distance into punching range, I hook my right hand over Chinzo's left hand to break his guard. It's important to notice how I step my right foot to the outside of his lead leg. This not only gives me a dominant angle of attack, but it also places my head outside of his line of fire.

3

As I lunge forward, I shift my weight onto my right leg, come up onto the ball of my left foot, pull my right shoulder back, rotate my hips in a clockwise direction, and throw a left cross toward Chinzo's face.

4

Having broken Chinzo's guard with my right hand trap, I land a left cross square to his chin.

5

After I land with the cross, I slide my rear foot forward and wrap my left hand around Chinzo's neck.

6

To keep Chinzo's weight on his heels, I extend my left hand into his neck. As I do this, I hook the heel of my right foot around the back of his left calf.

7

Pushing Chinzo back and toward my right using my left hand, I sweep my right leg into the back of his left leg. At the same time, I latch on to his left wrist with my right hand and pull his arm toward me. The combination of these actions sends Chinzo plummeting toward the mat.

As Chinzo falls to his back, I plant my right foot on the mat.

To capitalize on Chinzo's stunned state, I cock my right arm back and prepare to throw a downward punch into his face.

As I drop my weight downward, I land a hard right hand to Chinzo's face.

I drop my left knee on Chinzo's chest to pin his shoulders to the mat. Once accomplished, I cock my right arm back and prepare to follow up my assault with more strikes.

Striking Attacks

STRIKING COMBINATION TO OUTSIDE FOOT SWEEP

In this sequence I demonstrate how to use a striking combination to set up an outside foot sweep when you and your opponent are in opposite fighting stances. Just as with the previous combo, the goal is to throw your strikes with intent to disrupt your opponent's balance and force his weight onto his back leg. If you throw lazy strikes, the sweep will be very difficult to manage. When studying the photos, pay special attention to my footwork. As I enter with my attack, I circle around to the outside of my opponent's lead leg. This provides me with a dominant angle of attack and allows me to throw a barrage of strikes that forces him to shift his weight onto his hind leg. Once I see this shift occur, I hook my lead foot around the back of his ankle and sweep his leg out from underneath him.

Technical Note: It's important to mention the difference between this foot sweep and the one demonstrated in the previous sequence. In the previous sequence, I swept my opponent to the mat by hooking the heel of my lead leg around my opponent's lead leg. In this sequence, I use the inside of my foot to sweep my opponent to the mat. The former should be performed anytime you are moving forward into your opponent's comfort zone with your hips partially squared with his hips. The technique demonstrated here should be implemented anytime you circle around to your opponent's side and secure a dominant angle of attack.

Chinzo has assumed a standard stance and I've assumed a southpaw stance. Both of us are searching for openings to attack.

Driving off the mat with my left foot, I step my right foot forward and toward my right. At the same time, I extend my left arm toward Chinzo's face as if I were throwing a cross.

3

Keeping my left arm extended to blind Chinzo from my next movement, I shift my weight onto my right leg and slide my left foot across the mat toward my right foot.

4

As I pull my left arm back, I grab Chinzo's left wrist with my right hand, transfer my weight onto my left leg, and begin rotating my hips in a counterclockwise direction.

5

To distract Chinzo from the kick and break his defense, I pull his left arm toward me using my right hand. With his left arm out of the picture, I lift my right knee toward my chest and circle my right foot around to the front of his left leg.

6

Unable to defend, I land a curving front kick to Chinzo's solar plexus.

7

I circle my right foot around the front of Chinzo's lead leg.

8

Still controlling Chinzo's left arm with my right hand, I step my right foot to the mat, rotate my body in a clockwise direction, and throw a left cross toward his chin.

9

Shifting my weight onto my right leg, I land a left cross to Chinzo's chin.

10

I pull my left arm back and reverse the rotation of my hips.

11

Having forced Chinzo's weight onto his heels, I am in a perfect position to execute a foot sweep. I accomplish this by pulling on his left arm with my right hand, shifting my weight onto my left leg, and hooking my right foot around the back of his left calf.

12

Sweeping my right leg toward my left side, I yank Chinzo's left leg out from underneath him.

13

As Chinzo falls to his back, I step my right foot to the mat.

14

I drop my left knee on Chinzo's chest, cock my left hand back, and prepare to drop a hard punch into his face.

FEINT KICK TO KICK SWEEP

After you've landed a couple of hard round kicks to your opponent's body and legs, chances are he will begin elevating his leg to check your round kicks. To use this reaction to your advantage, step to the outside of his centerline as if you are going to throw a powerful round kick with your rear leg. As he raises his leg to check what he thinks to be a round kick, quickly step your rear leg forward to switch your stance and kick his grounded leg using your opposite leg. When you time your shot correctly, you will sweep your opponent's leg out from underneath him and put him on his back, giving you a number of attack options.

Chinzo has assumed a standard stance and I've assumed a southpaw stance. Both of us are searching for openings to attack.

To fake a rear round kick, I drive off the mat using my left foot and take a large outward step with my right foot. As I shift my weight onto my right leg, I rotate my hips and shoulders in a clockwise direction, extend my left arm, and slide my left foot across the mat as if I were going to throw a left round kick. Deceived by my actions, Chinzo elevates his left knee to block the strike.

As Chinzo lifts his left knee to his chest to block what he thinks is a left round kick, I drive off the mat with my right foot, step my left foot forward, and reverse the rotation of my hips. As I turn my body toward my left, I reach my right arm across his body.

Before Chinzo can bring his left leg down to reestablish his stance, I sweep my right leg underneath his left leg, striking the back of his right leg with my right instep. At the same time, I place my right hand on his chest and push him backward. It's important to note the angle at which my leg travels. Unlike a standard round kick, this kick follows an upward trajectory, much like kicking a soccer ball.

I kick Chinzo's right leg out from underneath him and send him plummeting toward the mat.

6

As Chinzo falls to his back, I step my right foot to the mat and cock my left hand back.

7

To capitalize on Chinzo's stunned state, I will throw a hard left punch to his face.

FEINT KICK TO OUTSIDE LEG TRIP

In this sequence I demonstrate how to feint a round kick to your opponent's head to set up an outside leg trip. Although the goal is not to land the round kick, you must throw it with enough intent to get your opponent to react. When executed properly, he will elevate his arms to protect his head. Instead of following through with the strike, you maneuver your kicking leg to the outside of his lead leg and plant your foot on the mat. To execute the sweep, all you have to do is push him over your leg as demonstrated below. The key to success with this technique is selling the round kick and then making a fluid transition to the outside trip.

Chinzo has assumed a standard stance and I've assumed a southpaw stance. Both of us are searching for openings to attack.

Driving off the mat with my left foot, I take a small step forward with my right foot, throw my left arm across my body, and start rotating my hips in a clockwise direction.

To fake the high round kick, I shift my weight onto my right leg and lift my left knee toward Chinzo's face. Notice how my actions cause him to elevate his arms to protect his head.

4

Having distracted Chinzo with the feint, I abandon the kick and maneuver my left leg around the outside of his left leg.

5

I hook my left leg around the back of Chinzo's left leg and then plant my foot to the inside of his right foot. At the same time, I wrap my left arm around the right side of his neck and grab his left arm with my right hand.

6

I pull on Chinzo's left arm with my right hand while pushing on the left side of his neck with my left hand. The combination of these actions forces his weight toward his left side. With my leg serving as a barrier that prevents him from stepping his left leg back to counterbalance his weight, he trips and begins falling toward the mat.

7

Chinzo continues to plummet to the mat.

Keeping my left hand pinned to the left side of Chinzo's neck, I guide him to the ground.

As Chinzo lands on his back, I cock my right hand back.

I bring my right arm down and deliver a hard punch to Chinzo's face.

PART TWO
INTERCEPTING ATTACKS

In this section I demonstrate a number of highly effective counterattacking techniques, all of which fall into one of two categories. The first category includes techniques that involve intercepting your opponent's attack, which is accomplished by launching your counter while he is in the middle of throwing his strike. For example, your opponent throws a rear round kick, and you counter with a right cross before his kick can land. As long as you spot the kick coming early, this interception is feasible because linear strikes such as the cross have less distance to travel than circular strikes such as the round kick. However, to successfully pull off these types of techniques, your timing, sense of distance, and reaction speed must be razor sharp. If you are off by even a fraction of a second, there is a good chance that you'll eat a powerful blow.

Although intercepting attacks involves some risk, it has many advantages. Most fighters are used to throwing a strike, hitting or missing their target, and then dealing with your counter to that strike. When you land your strike while he is in the middle of throwing his strike, you often disrupt his striking rhythm, which creates an opportunity for you to immediately follow up with a combination. In addition to this, hitting your opponent while he is moving forward drastically increases the power of your shot.

Intercepting attacks is ideal, but not always possible. If your opponent catches you off guard or you're out of position when he attacks, it's often best to employ one of the techniques in the second category, which focuses on evading your opponent's strike and then launching your counter. The goal with these techniques is to cause your opponent to miss his strike and then capitalize on his awkward positioning with a strike of your own. If you allow him to pull his arm

or leg back toward his body and reestablish his fighting stance before initiating your attack, there is a good chance that you will walk straight into his secondary strike. To prevent such an outcome, it is important to drill these techniques as much as possible to increase your reaction speed.

As you flip through the coming pages, you will notice that I do not demonstrate the traditional blocking techniques that are taught in the majority of karate dojos. Personally, I try not to block strikes using my arms or legs. In Machida Karate-Do, the goal is to inflict as much damage as possible without taking any abuse in the process. While blocking strikes is certainly better than getting hit, you still absorb the impact of the blow. Blocking also hinders your movement, which oftentimes allows your opponent to follow up with more strikes. By either intercepting his attack or evading his strikes and then countering, you make him pay for his aggression. This strips him of his confidence and makes him hesitant to attack. If neither option is possible for whatever reason, simply getting out of the way of his strike is your next best move. I personally feel that blocking should only be employed when you have no other choice.

2-1: Intercepting Kicks

In this section I demonstrate how to intercept and counter your opponent's kicks. As I have already mentioned, to be successful with these techniques you must time your counter so that you land your strike before your opponent can complete the motion of his kick. If your timing is off, not only will you eat a powerful kick, but you will also most likely get knocked off balance, which compromises your position and makes you vulnerable to your opponent's secondary attack. To prevent this outcome, you must study your opponent's movements and pick up on his tendencies. For example, a lot of fighters will square their shoulders before throwing a kick. Instead of waiting for him to hurl his leg toward your body, the instant you see this small movement, you initiate your counter. As you will see in the coming techniques, it is also important to move your body in the same direction that your opponent's kick is heading. This not only increases the distance his kick has to travel to connect with your body, but it also reduces the power of his kick should it land. Intercepting kicks is not easy, especially when you are up against a good kickboxer, but if you take the time to master these stealthy counters, you will become a very difficult fighter to hit.

2-2: Intercepting Punches

Intercepting hand strikes is the same as intercepting kicks in that you must land your counterattack before your opponent can complete his punch. Just as with intercepting kicks, you want to move in the same direction as your opponent's punch. For example, if he throws a circular punch such as a hook or overhand, you move in the same lateral direction to increase the distance his fist has to travel to hit your body or face. If he throws a linear punch, you have a couple of options. With punches being thrown from close range, one option is to step back to remove your body from the danger zone, and then move into your opponent and launch your counter before he can reestablish his fighting stance. The second option is to move to the outside of his line of fire and throw your counterstrike at the same time. With both options, the key to success is not to depend upon your eyes alone. You must feel

your opponent's strike coming. Like countering kicks, you must study all of your opponent's movements, looking for signs that give a particular strike away. If you notice that he has the tendency to cock his hand back every time he throws a cross, you can get the jump on him again and again.

2-3: Takedown Defense

In this section I demonstrate how to evade, counter, and intercept your opponent's takedown attempts, as well as how to attain the top position should he manage to shoot past your defensive lines and obtain control of your body. Even if your goal is to take your opponent to the mat, it is imperative that you learn takedown defense because it allows you to dictate the course of the fight.

Just as with intercepting punches and kicks, you must be able to distinguish your opponent's takedown attacks and employ the appropriate counter. For example, if he shoots in from a distance, you have the option of intercepting his forward penetration with a knee or uppercut. However, if he manages to get past your defensive lines by shooting in from close range or setting his takedown up with strikes, you may have to sprawl your legs back and drive your hips to the mat to avoid it. Again, developing your timing, sense of distance, and reaction speed is key to being successful with your counters. If you hesitate, you will most likely end up on your back with your opponent on top of you, which is not a favorable outcome.

INTERCEPT ROUND KICK WITH SWITCH-STEP LUNGE-PUNCH

In this sequence I demonstrate how to counter your opponent's rear round kick utilizing a switch step and a lunge-punch. The goal is to reverse the positioning of your feet the instant your opponent launches his attack, and then explode forward with the cross. The combination of these two actions changes your angle of attack, not only making it difficult for your opponent to land his kick, but also creating an opening to land your punch. The key to success is moving with your opponent. If you delay with your countering movements, the chances that you will land your punch before your opponent lands his kick drop dramatically. Although this type of technique is popular in karate, it is not very common in other styles. If your goal is to be a dangerous counterstriker, I strongly suggest adding this technique and others like it into your arsenal. It is important to mention that this particular counter should only be used when your opponent throws a rear round kick from the same fighting stance. Later in the section I demonstrate how to counter the rear round kick when you are in opposite stances.

Chinzo and I are in standard stances with our left foot forward. Both of us are searching for an opening to attack.

Chinzo initiates a rear round kick. In order to evade and counter his kick from the same stance, I first have to reverse the positioning of my feet so that I can enter with my opposite leg and hand. To begin this process, I slide my left foot back to my rear foot and then shift a larger portion of my weight onto my left leg.

Having switched my stance, I drive off the mat using my left foot and lunge forward with a straight right punch.

I drive my right fist into Chinzo's face before he can complete the rotation of his hips and land his round kick. In case your timing is off, it's important that you elevate your opposite arm as I demonstrate here.

INTERCEPT ROUND KICK WITH ROUND KICK

This is another technique that you can utilize when your opponent throws a rear round kick from the same stance. As in the previous sequence, I evade my opponent's kick by retracting my lead leg, but instead of lunging forward with my rear leg and throwing a cross, I throw a rear round kick to his abdomen. If you look at the photos below, you'll notice that I keep my hips square with my opponent as I switch my stance. This is very important. If you move your center of gravity as you step back, not only will you compromise your balance, but you will also lose power in your kick. When you utilize proper form and land the strike clean, your opponent will most likely get knocked backward. To capitalize on his awkward positioning, an excellent option is to drop your kicking leg to the mat and follow up with a straight punch as demonstrated below.

Chinzo and I are in standard stances with our left foot forward. Both of us are searching for an opening to attack.

Chinzo opens his hips to throw a rear round kick. Keen to his intentions, I slide my left foot back and prepare to counter.

Shifting my weight onto my left leg, I lean my upper body slightly back, pull my left shoulder back, and rotate my hips in a counterclockwise direction. At the same time, I coil my right heel to my right buttock and extend my right arm for balance. To protect the left side of my body and head from the kick, I keep my left arm elevated.

I extend my right leg and drive the ball of my right foot into Chinzo's stomach.

With Chinzo off balance and stunned from the kick, I recoil my leg, step my foot toward the mat, and fire a jab toward his exposed face.

Using the momentum of my downward step to my advantage, I land a powerful right jab to Chinzo's face.

INTERCEPTING KICKS

INTERCEPT ROUND KICK WITH CROSS

In this sequence I demonstrate how to intercept a rear low kick with a cross when you are squared off with your opponent in an opposite stance. When studying the photos, pay special attention to the timing of the strike. I start my attack the instant my opponent initiates his attack, and I land the punch before he can complete the rotation of his kick. In order to apply this counter, you have to train the technique tirelessly in the gym until the movements become instinctual. Remember, the idea is not to see the strike coming but to feel it coming. If you are slow to react or hesitate for only a split second, this counter will not work.

Chinzo has assumed a standard stance and I've assumed a southpaw stance. Both of us are searching for openings to attack.

Chinzo takes a small step forward with his left foot and begins rotating his hips and shoulders in a counterclockwise direction. Keen to his intentions, I immediately counter by stepping my right foot to the outside of his left foot. It's important that you jump into action the moment your opponent telegraphs the kick. If there is any hesitation or your timing is off by a fraction of a second, then you risk getting hit with the strike.

As Chinzo rotates his body to throw a rear round kick, I come up onto the ball of my left foot, pull my right shoulder back, rotate my hips in a clockwise direction, and throw a left cross toward his face.

Continuing with my previous movements, I drive my left fist into the right side of Chinzo's jaw. It's important to note that a straight strike takes less time to reach its target than a circular one. As a result, my fist collides with my opponent's face before he can he can complete the rotation of his kick.

INTERCEPT ROUND KICK WITH CROSS TO LOW-KICK SWEEP

When you manage to intercept your opponent's round kick with a powerful cross, the impact from the blow will most likely knock him backward. An excellent way to capitalize on his shattered base is to follow up with a sweeping kick to his grounded leg. If your timing is correct, you will rip his grounded leg out from underneath him and cause him to collapse to the mat.

Chinzo has assumed a standard stance and I've assumed a southpaw stance. Both of us are searching for openings to attack.

Chinzo takes a small step forward with his left foot and begins rotating his hips and shoulders in a counterclockwise direction. With a small window of opportunity in which to counter, I step my right foot to the outside of his left foot and prepare to launch a straight left cross toward his face. It's important that you jump into action the moment your opponent telegraphs the kick. If there is any hesitation or your timing is off by a fraction of a second, then the counter will not work.

As Chinzo rotates his body to throw the rear round kick, I turn my hips in a clockwise direction, pull my right shoulder back, and land a left cross to his chin. Notice that as I land with the cross, I slide my left foot up. This puts me in range to land a left low kick to his grounded left leg.

Having landed the cross, I continue to rotate my hips in a clockwise direction and drive my fist into Chinzo's face to force him backward. As I do this, I turn my right foot so that my toes are pointing toward my right side. This primes my hips to throw a left kick.

Before Chinzo can step his right leg to the mat to reestablish his base, I throw a sweeping left round kick to the back of his left knee. It's important to note that I throw the cross and then the kick in one fluid motion, never stopping the rotation of my hips.

Following through with my left leg kick, I sweep Chinzo's grounded leg out from underneath.

Chinzo plummets to the mat.

As Chinzo collapses to his back, I step my left foot to the mat, reassume my fighting stance, and start plotting my attack from the top position.

INTERCEPTING KICKS

INTERCEPT ROUND KICK WITH SPINNING BACK KICK

The spinning back kick is another excellent technique for counting your opponent's rear round kick when you are in opposite fighting stances. However, it is important to mention that successfully pulling off this counter requires razor-sharp timing and a keen sense of distance. The goal is to rotate your body the instant you sense the kick coming, and then lash out with your linear strike before your opponent can land his circular strike. It is an advanced technique because it requires you to take your eyes off your opponent and turn your back to him for a split second, but by tirelessly working on developing your speed and accuracy during training, you can make it a very effective counterstrike.

Technical Note: This strike is best applied to counter your opponent's high round kick as opposed to a low round kick. As you know, it takes longer for the high round kick to reach its target than the low kick, which gives you a little more time to execute your counter.

Chinzo has assumed a standard stance and I've assumed a southpaw stance. Both of us are searching for openings to attack.

As Chinzo opens his hips to throw a rear round kick, I pivot on my lead foot and start rotating my body in a counterclockwise direction.

Still turning my body in a counterclockwise direction, I shift my weight onto my right leg, turn my head to get an eye on my target, lean my upper body forward to counterbalance my weight, and coil my left heel toward my left buttock.

Using the momentum of my counterclockwise turn to my advantage, I drive my left heel into Chinzo's stomach before he can connect with his round kick.

INTERCEPT REAR PUNCH WITH OVERHAND

In this sequence I demonstrate how to counter your opponent's rear-handed strike by utilizing a back step and an overhand punch. Just as with the previous technique, the goal is to sense the punch coming and immediately employ your counter-movement. When timed correctly, you land your punch before your opponent can land his, thwarting his attack. Personally, I like to employ this technique against opponents who constantly press forward. It halts them dead in their tracks and does wonders to curb their aggression.

Technical Note: It's important to note that this technique works when your opponent advances straight forward with a rear punch, whether it is a straight cross, an overhand, or a rear hook as shown below. It's also important to note that you are not limited to countering with just the overhand. You have the option of throwing the straight cross or even an uppercut. The technique you utilize should be based on the technique your opponent is using and the positioning of your body.

Chinzo and I are in standard stances with our left foot forward. Both of us are searching for an opening to attack.

Chinzo lunges forward to throw a rear punch. To maintain separation and position myself to counter, I slide my left foot back.

3

I shift my weight onto my left leg and step my right leg back.

4

As I step my right foot behind me, I pull my left shoulder back, rotate my hips in a counterclockwise direction, and throw a right overhand toward Chinzo's face. In case my timing is off, I've positioned my left hand at eye level to protect the left side of my face.

5

Continuing with my previous actions, I plant the ball of my right foot on the mat, turn my fist over so that my right thumb is facing the ground, and drive the knuckles of my index and middle fingers into the left side of Chinzo's jaw.

INTERCEPT CROSS WITH FRONT KICK TO JAB TO CROSS

This is another technique that can be used when your opponent advances forward with a rear punch. It is similar to the previous technique in that you slide your lead foot back the instant you see the punch coming, but instead of using that newly created distance to throw a cross, you use it to throw a rear front kick into your opponent's midsection. When you land the kick clean, you not only halt his forward progression, but you also cause his body to double over and his hands to drop. This creates a perfect opening to follow up with more strikes. In this particular sequence, I chose to finish the combination with a jab and then a cross. When studying the photos, it is important to notice that immediately after landing the kick I drop my foot to the outside of my opponent's lead leg. This gives me a dominant angle of attack and removes my body from his line of fire.

Chinzo and I are in standard stances with our left foot forward. Both of us are searching for an opening to attack.

Chinzo lunges forward to throw a rear punch. To maintain separation and position myself to counter, I slide my left foot back.

Keeping my hips square with my opponent, I shift my weight onto my left leg, elevate my right knee, and curl my right heel to my right buttock.

Before Chinzo can connect with his strike, I thrust my hips forward, lean my upper body slightly back, extend my right leg, and drive the ball of my right foot into his solar plexus.

Having stopped Chinzo dead in his tracks with the front kick, I recoil my leg and prepare to follow up with more strikes.

To capitalize on Chinzo's stunned state, I step my right foot to the mat and land a right jab to his chin. Notice how I acquire a dominant angle of attack by posting my right foot to the outside of his lead leg.

I pull my right hand back into my stance and prepare to launch a left cross.

Pulling my right shoulder back and rotating my hips in a clockwise direction, I throw a left cross to Chinzo's jaw.

INTERCEPT REAR HOOK WITH CROSS TO LEAD HOOK

In this sequence I demonstrate how to intercept your opponent's rear hook using a cross when in opposite fighting stances. To be successful with this technique, the instant you see your opponent put his punch into motion, step your lead foot to the outside of his lead leg and fire your cross straight down his centerline. With straight punches having to travel less distance to reach their target than circular ones, you land your punch prior to your opponent landing his, thwarting his attack. Once you deliver the cross, you will usually be in a good position to follow up with more strikes. In this particular sequence, I choose to keep my offense going by throwing a lead hook to my opponent's jaw.

Chinzo has assumed a standard stance and I've assumed a southpaw stance. Both of us are searching for openings to attack.

Chinzo telegraphs a right punch by cocking his right hand back and stepping his left foot forward. To counter, I drive off my left foot and step my right foot forward and to the outside of his left leg. At the same time, I pull my right shoulder back, rotate my hips in a clockwise direction, and throw a left cross toward his face.

Continuing with my previous actions, I land a left cross to Chinzo's face.

While Chinzo is stunned from the cross, I immediately follow up my attack by throwing a right hook. To initiate this action, I draw my left hand back into my stance, pull my left shoulder back, rotate my hips in a counterclockwise direction, and throw my right arm along a circular arc toward Chinzo's face. To protect the left side of my face from counterstrikes, I've elevated my left hand to eye level.

Still pulling my left shoulder back and rotating my hips in a counterclockwise direction, I drive the first two knuckles of my right hand into the left side of Chinzo's jaw.

INTERCEPT REAR HOOK WITH CROSS TO FRONT KICK TO CROSS

As I mention numerous times throughout this book, you never want to attack or counter with a predetermined combination. The strikes you choose to employ in a combination should be based upon your opponent's reactions to your initial strike or movement. For example, in the sequence below my opponent charges forward with a rear hook from an opposite fighting stance, and I counter with a straight cross—the exact same situation that was demonstrated in the previous sequence. However, in this scenario my cross forces my opponent backward, putting him out of range to land with a lead hook. Instead of throwing a lead hook and missing, I alter my combination and throw a rear front kick to his midsection. With my front kick doubling my opponent over and momentarily dropping his guard, his face is once again vulnerable to attack. To capitalize on that vulnerability, I step my kicking leg to the mat and follow up with another cross. Instead of choreographing your attacks, let instinct dictate the strikes that you throw. Although this can take a long time to master, it will make you a very dangerous fighter in the long run.

Chinzo has assumed a standard stance and I've assumed a southpaw stance. Both of us are searching for openings to attack.

Chinzo telegraphs a right punch by cocking his right hand back and stepping his left foot forward. To counter, I drive off my left foot and step my right foot forward and to the outside of his lead leg. At the same time, I pull my right shoulder back, rotate my hips in a clockwise direction, and throw a left cross toward his face.

Continuing with my previous actions, I land a left cross to Chinzo's face.

The impact from the cross forces Chinzo backward, creating separation between our bodies. To capitalize, I shift my weight onto my right leg, elevate my left knee, curl my left heel toward my buttock, and prepare to launch a left front kick to his midsection.

Leaning back slightly and extending my leg, I drive the ball of my left foot into Chinzo's solar plexus.

To avoid falling forward after landing with the front kick, I recoil my leg by pulling my left heel toward my left buttock.

Instead of stepping my left leg back into my stance, I drive off my rear leg, drop my left foot to the mat, and prepare to follow up with a right cross.

Transferring my weight onto my left leg, I come up onto the ball of my right foot, pull my left shoulder back, rotate my hips in a counterclockwise direction, and throw a right cross to Chinzo's face. Notice how I've kept my left hand elevated to protect the left side of my face from counterstrikes.

INTERCEPT REAR HOOK WITH CROSS TO TAKEDOWN DEFENSE

This is the same scenario that was presented in the previous two sequences. Your opponent launches a rear hook from an opposite fighting stance, and you counter with a powerful cross to his face. However, in this scenario your opponent doesn't hold his ground or move backward upon getting hit with the cross, which eliminates your ability to land either the rear hook or front kick. Instead, he drives forward in an attempt to tie you up in the clinch and execute a takedown, a common reaction with fighters who have a wrestling background. Continuing with a predetermined attack in this situation would almost surely allow your opponent to be successful with his goal. To prevent him from tying you up in the clinch, you must adapt your attack to his reaction. This can be accomplished by wrapping your arms around his head, positioning your elbows in front of his shoulders, and then pulling him off balance using your newly established grip. Once you have broken his base in this fashion, you will be in a good position to follow up with more strikes, as demonstrated below. Remember, you never know how your opponent is going to react when hurt. As long as you remain relaxed and focused on his reactions, you will almost always be able to keep the upper hand.

Chinzo has assumed a standard stance and I've assumed a southpaw stance. Both of us are searching for openings to attack.

Chinzo telegraphs a right punch by cocking his right hand back and stepping forward with his left leg. To counter, I drive off my rear leg and step my right foot forward and to the outside of his left leg. At the same time, I pull my right shoulder back, rotate my hips in a clockwise direction, and throw a left cross toward his face.

3

Continuing with my previous actions, I land a left cross to Chinzo's face.

4

Stunned from the cross, Chinzo leans forward and attempts to tie me up in the clinch. To prevent him from accomplishing his goal, I wrap both of my arms around the back of his head and position my elbows in front of his shoulders.

5

To capitalize on Chinzo's forward energy, I pivot on my right foot, turn my body in a counterclockwise direction, slide my left foot circularly across the mat, and pull down on his head with both of my arms. Notice the combination of the actions forces Chinzo off balance.

6

Still pulling on Chinzo's head, I slide my right foot back.

I continue to pull Chinzo in a counterclockwise direction. Notice how he is forced to counterbalance his weight with a sideways step.

With Chinzo off balance and discombobulated, I release my grip on his head and push him away.

Before Chinzo can reestablish his stance, I shift my weight onto my left leg, elevate my right knee, and pull my right heel toward my right buttock.

10

I throw a right front kick to Chinzo's abdomen.

11

Staying balanced on my left leg, I recoil my right leg.

12

I drop my right foot to the mat and then shift my weight onto my right leg. Next, I come up onto the ball of my left foot, pull my right shoulder back, rotate my hips in a clockwise direction, and throw a left cross to the right side of Chinzo's jaw.

INTERCEPT CROSS WITH LEAD HOOK TO UPPERCUT TO KNEE

In this sequence I demonstrate how to counter your opponent's cross using a lead hook when in opposite fighting stances. The most important aspect of this technique is circling to the outside of your opponent's lead leg the instant he fires off his punch. With the cross being a linear punch and the hook being a circular one, the cross will most likely land first if you stand directly in front of your opponent. However, by pivoting on your lead foot and sliding your rear foot circularly across the mat as you throw the hook, you not only remove your body from your opponent's line of fire, but you also acquire a dominant angle of attack. This dominant angle creates an opening to land the hook, and it also allows you to immediately follow up with more strikes once the hook has landed. In this particular scenario, I personally like to follow up with a rear uppercut and then a knee strike. When studying the photos, it is important to notice how each attack flows into the next. The right hook opens your opponent up for the left uppercut, and the left uppercut sets him up for the devastating knee strike. As I mentioned before, basing your strikes upon the openings made available is essential to becoming a master striker.

Chinzo has assumed a standard stance and I've assumed a southpaw stance. Both of us are searching for openings to attack.

Chinzo initiates an attack by stepping his left foot forward. Immediately I step my right foot forward and to the outside of his lead foot.

As I step with my right foot, I pull my left shoulder back, rotate my hips in a counterclockwise direction, and throw a right hook toward the left side of Chinzo's face. It's important to notice that by stepping my foot to the outside of my opponent's lead leg, I've effectively removed my head from his line of fire. It's also important to notice that I've kept my left hand elevated to protect the left side of my face.

Still rotating my body in a counterclockwise direction, I plant my right foot to the mat, slide my left foot circularly across the mat, and drive the first two knuckles of my right fist into the left side of Chinzo's jaw. Notice how my actions cause him to miss with his strike.

As I draw my right hand back toward my body, I shift a portion of my weight onto my right leg, pull my right shoulder back, rotate my hips in a clockwise direction, come up onto the ball of my left foot, and throw a left uppercut upward between Chinzo's guard.

6

I land a left uppercut to Chinzo's chin.

7

Instead of retracting my punching arm, I reach my left hand to the left side of Chinzo's head. At the same time, I grab his left wrist with my right hand.

8

I wrap my left hand around the left side of Chinzo's head, and then use my control to pull his head down into my left knee. To prevent him from blocking the strike, I pull down on his right arm using my left hand. It's important to note that although I am landing the knee to my opponent's face, you have the option of throwing it to his midsection. The option you choose should be based upon the opening that is available.

INTERCEPT JAB WITH RIDGEHAND TO KNEE-PICK TAKEDOWN

In this sequence I demonstrate how to counter your opponent's jab with a ridgehand strike when in opposite fighting stances. Just as with the previous technique, you must step your lead foot to the outside of your opponent's lead foot the instant he launches his jab. This removes your head from the path of his linear strike, as well as provides you with the angle you need to land your circular strike. Although the ridgehand is an excellent weapon to employ in this scenario, it can be replaced with an overhand punch by closing your hand and striking with the knuckles of your index and middle fingers. With both options, you will usually be in an excellent position to transition into the knee-pick takedown immediately after landing your strike. To accomplish this, do not pull your striking arm back into your stance. Instead, hook your arm across your opponent's neck and drive him backward. At the same time, chop his lead leg out from underneath him using your opposite hand. By pushing his upper body in one direction and his lower body in the other direction, your opponent has no choice but to collapse to the mat. It is important to mention that although I apply this technique as a counter in the sequence below, it can also be utilized as an attack.

Chinzo has assumed a standard stance and I've assumed a southpaw stance. Both of us are searching for openings to attack.

Chinzo throws a straight jab at my face. As he extends his arm, I step my right foot to the outside of his left foot, come up onto the ball of my left foot, rotate my body in a clockwise direction, and whip my left arm along a circular arc toward his face. Notice how my outward step removes my head from his line of fire.

3

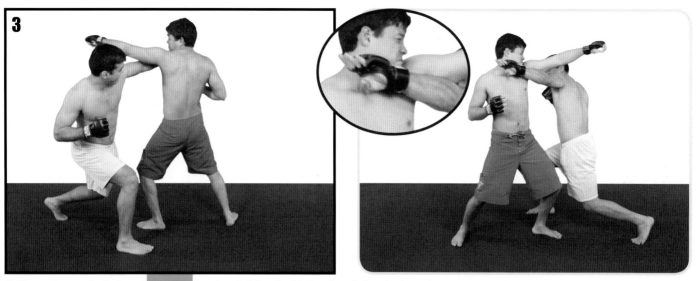

Still rotating my body in a clockwise direction, I drive the blade of my left wrist into the right side of Chinzo's jaw.

4

Having stunned Chinzo with the ridgehand strike, I wrap my left hand around his neck and start pushing him toward my right. At the same time, I chop my right hand into the back of his left leg.

5

Still pushing Chinzo toward my right side using my left arm, I sweep his left leg out from underneath him with my right hand. Unable to counterbalance his weight with a backward step, he begins plummeting to the mat.

6

As Chinzo falls to the mat, I slide my left leg forward.

7

I drop my left knee on Chinzo's left side and cock my right arm back.

8

I drop my weight and drive my right fist into Chinzo's face.

JAB TO UPPERCUT (COUNTER LEVEL CHANGE)

The majority of fighters realize the importance of setting up their takedowns. Sometimes they will distract you with a combination of strikes, and other times they will set up their takedowns by evading one of your strikes. In this scenario my opponent chooses the latter. As I throw a jab at his face, he drops his elevation to evade my punch and then immediately shoots his body forward in an attempt to gain control of my legs. To prevent him from accomplishing his goal, I rotate my hips and throw a rear uppercut to his chin, halting his forward progression and causing him a significant amount of damage. The key to being successful with this technique is spotting your opponent's elevation drop and then immediately reacting to it by throwing the uppercut. If your opponent manages to close the distance between your bodies before you can land the punch, sprawling your legs back and dropping your hips to the mat is the preferred option. Later in this section I demonstrate how to perform this method of defense.

Chinzo and I are in standard stances with our left foot forward. Both of us are searching for an opening to attack.

To setup my attack, I throw a left jab toward Chinzo's face. As I extend my arm, Chinzo drops his level and evades the strike by ducking his head underneath the punch.

Having spotted his level change, I lower my right arm, dip my right shoulder toward the mat, bend my right knee, and come up onto the ball of my right foot. At the same time, I pull my left shoulder back and rotate my hips in a counterclockwise direction.

Continuing with my previous movements, I extend my arm along an upward arc and drive my fist into Chinzo's chin.

INTERCEPT SHOT WITH KNEE

This technique is similar to the previous one in that your opponent drops his elevation to shoot in for a takedown, and you halt his forward progression with a hard strike before he can gain control of your legs. However, instead of throwing a rear uppercut, you throw a rear knee. Again, timing is crucial in order to pull this technique off successfully. You must perceive your opponent's level change, and then immediately fire off the knee strike before he can close the distance between you. Personally, I find this technique works best in the later rounds of a fight, especially when you have been able to outscore your opponent on your feet. Frustrated and fatigued, many fighters will begin advancing forward with reckless abandon in an attempt to take you to the ground. When the forward momentum of your opponent's body meets the forward momentum of your knee, it often produces a dramatic knockout.

Chinzo and I are in standard stances with our left foot forward. Both of us are searching for an opening to attack.

In an attempt to secure a takedown, Chinzo steps forward while lowering his elevation. Immediately I shift my weight onto my left leg, rotate my body in a counterclockwise direction, and extend my right arm.

Still rotating my hips in a counterclockwise direction, I throw a right straight knee between Chinzo's guard and toward his face.

I drive my right knee into Chinzo's face. To increase the power of the strike, I use my right hand to guide his face downward into the knee.

TAKEDOWN DEFENSE

INTERCEPT SHOT WITH MUAY THAI CLINCH

If you get caught off guard or your feet are in an awkward position when your opponent drops his elevation, attempting to halt his forward progression with a rear uppercut or knee strike can make you even more vulnerable to the takedown. In such a situation, a much better option is to position your elbows in front of his shoulders and cup your hands together behind his head, securing the Muay Thai clinch. With your elbows preventing your opponent from continuing to drive forward, you can sprawl your hips away from his reach. Once you have created distance in this fashion, not only will your opponent have a difficult time completing the takedown, but you will also be in a good position to deliver a knee strike to his midsection or face.

Chinzo and I are in standard stances with our left foot forward. Both of us are searching for an opening to attack.

Chinzo drops his elevation and shoots in for a takedown. Unable to counter with a strike, I immediately maneuver both of my arms to the front of his shoulders.

Keeping my elbows positioned in front of Chinzo's shoulders to prevent him from driving forward, I slide my left foot and hips back to prevent him from grabbing my legs.

Having effectively stopped the takedown with my previous actions, I grip my hands together behind Chinzo's head and slide my right foot back.

Using my control to guide Chinzo's head down, I throw a right knee to his midsection. When executing this step, it's important that you keep your elbows positioned in front of his shoulders upon landing with the strike. This will prevent your opponent from ducking underneath your arms and securing control of your hips as you retract your leg.

KNEE TO SINGLE-LEG ESCAPE

In the previous sequence I demonstrated how to avoid your opponent's takedown by securing the Muay Thai clinch and driving a rear knee into his sternum. Although this is an excellent technique that often results in a knockdown, sometimes your opponent will wrap his arms around your leg as you throw the knee in an attempt to secure a single-leg takedown. If you should find yourself in this scenario, employing the single-leg escape demonstrated below is an excellent option.

Chinzo and I are in standard stances with our left foot forward. Both of us are searching for an opening to attack.

Chinzo lowers his elevation to shoot in for a takedown. Unable to counter with a strike due to our close proximity, I immediately maneuver both of my arms in front of his shoulders and slide my right leg back.

Having stopped Chinzo's forward progression with my previous actions, I grip my hands together around the back of his head and prepare to launch a knee toward his midsection.

As I lift my right knee to land the strike, Chinzo wraps both of his arms around my right leg.

Chinzo manages to wrap his arms around my right leg and secure the single-leg position.

Before Chinzo can initiate an attack from the single-leg position, I maneuver my right foot to the front of his left leg, and position my right palm on the back of his head.

Here I am doing several things at once. I push Chinzo's head toward the mat with my right arm, turn my body in a counterclockwise direction, and drop my right knee toward the mat. At the same time, I begin pulling my right leg in the direction of my counterclockwise turn.

I pull my trapped leg free as I continue with my previous actions.

Keeping my right hand pinned to the back of Chinzo's head to maintain distance, I step my right foot to the mat. Note, by maintaining space in this manner you prevent your opponent from closing the distance and securing control of your back as you escape the position.

I reestablish my fighting stance and start plotting my next attack.

SPRAWL TO STANDING

Earlier in this section I demonstrated how to avoid your opponent's shot using strikes, as well as how to stop his forward progression by securing the Muay Thai clinch. Although both of these techniques are preferred methods of defense, they aren't always possible. If you are fighting an explosive wrestler, there is a good chance that he will manage to penetrate through both of these defensive lines. In such a scenario, employing a sprawl is oftentimes your best chance of avoiding the takedown. To accomplish this, hook your arms around the front of your opponent's near shoulder, shoot your legs behind you, drop your hips to the mat, and plant your chest on his back. The combination of these actions redirects his forward momentum down into the mat, preventing him from reaching your legs and executing the takedown. Once accomplished, you have the option of obtaining a more dominant position on the ground or immediately working your way back to your feet, which I demonstrate in the sequence below.

Chinzo and I are in standard stances with our left foot forward. Both of us are searching for an opening to attack.

Chinzo lowers his elevation and shoots in for a takedown. Unable to counter with a strike or stuff his shot with my elbows, I lower my guard and begin dropping my level.

I stuff Chinzo's shot by catching his left arm and shoulders in the crook of my arms. At the same time, I drop my chest forward and sprawl my legs back.

4

I drop my hips and redirect Chinzo's forward energy down into the mat.

5

Wasting no time, I place my right hand on Chinzo's left shoulder and start working my way back up to my feet.

6

Keeping my right hand pinned on Chinzo's shoulder to maintain distance, I pop up to my feet.

7

I reestablish my fighting stance.

SPRAWL TO STANDING (OPPOSITE STANCE)

While double-leg takedowns are common when you and your opponent are in the same fighting stance, single-leg take-downs are more prevalent when you are in opposite fighting stances. This is partially due to the fact that your lead leg is positioned so close to your opponent's lead leg, making it easy for him to grab your leg and hoist it up to his chest. Although there are many ways to defend against the single, utilizing a sprawl is one of the safest. If you look at the photos below, you'll notice that my opponent shoots in with his head positioned to the inside of my body. To suppress his attack, I drive my rear arm in front of his rear shoulder, throw my legs back, drop my hips to the mat, and collapse my chest over the back of his shoulders. Unlike when defending against the double-leg, I am unable to simply stand up from this position. With my opponent's head positioned to the inside of my body, if I began climbing to my feet, he could immediately shoot in for another takedown. To prevent this outcome, the instant I block his shot I throw my arm over his back and spin around to his side. This gives me numerous options. If my goal is to keep the fight on the ground, I could remain on top and work to secure control of my opponent's back. If my goal is to return to my feet, I can stand up and back away or climb to my feet and deliver a kick or knee to my opponent's body.

Chinzo has assumed a standard stance and I've assumed a southpaw stance. Both of us are searching for openings to attack.

Chinzo lowers his elevation and shoots in for a single-leg takedown.

3

To keep Chinzo from reaching my legs, I maneuver my left arm to the inside of his right shoulder and sprawl my legs back.

4

I stuff Chinzo's shot by catching his right shoulder in the crook of my left arm and by pressing in on his left arm using my right hand. At the same time, I collapse my chest over the top of his back and redirect his energy into the ground.

5

Wasting no time, I wrap my right arm over Chinzo's back and start circling toward his left side.

6

Still circling toward Chinzo's left side, I plant my right knee on the mat between his left arm and left leg and clamp my right arm around his right side.

7

Using my right arm to pin Chinzo to my body, I post my left foot on the mat and cock my left arm back. It's important to note that I am distributing a large portion of my weight over my opponent's back. This makes it very difficult for him to escape the position by standing up.

8

I drive my fist into the left side of Chinzo's face. From here, I can continue my assault from top control or work my way back up to my feet. In this particular situation, I choose the latter.

9

I place my hands on Chinzo's back and start climbing up to my feet.

10

I step my right leg back and stand up. From here, I have the option of reestablishing my stance or delivering a kick or knee to Chinzo's body.

PREVENTING THE SINGLE-LEG TAKEDOWN

Although sprawling is an excellent way to prevent your opponent from gaining control of your lead leg when he shoots in for a single, it isn't always possible. In this sequence, I demonstrate how to defend against the single when your opponent catches you off guard and manages to wrap his arms around your lead leg. If you look at the first photo below, you'll notice that he has his head pinned to my stomach and his hands positioned high up on my hips. This is the ideal position for him to attack. To neutralize his offense, I push his head toward the mat, which in turn causes his grip to slide down toward my knee. Having created distance between our bodies, I immediately secure an overhook on his near arm and circle my captured leg to the outside of his lead leg. Once accomplished, my opponent's hold on my leg is dramatically weakened, giving me the option of either driving my foot straight down to the mat or employing the single-leg escape previously shown.

Chinzo has my right leg trapped and is working for a single-leg takedown.

To eliminate his leverage and nullify his attacks, I place my hands on the top of his head and push it down and away from my body.

Maintaining downward pressure on Chinzo's head with my left hand, I wedge my right hand to the inside of his left arm.

Staying balanced on my left leg, I secure a right overhook on Chinzo's left arm and circle my right foot around his left leg.

I push outward on Chinzo's head with my left hand while pulling up on his left arm with my right overhook. At the same time, I hook my right foot around the outside of his left leg and then extend my leg into his leg. In most cases, the combination of these actions will force your opponent to release your leg. If he should maintain his hold, you can force your right foot to the mat or pull your leg free utilizing the single-leg escape shown previously in this section.

PART THREE
THE CLINCH

It doesn't matter if you have flawless movement and pinpoint accuracy with your punches and kicks—there will come a time when you find yourself tied up in the clinch, making it imperative that you spend an ample amount of time training to dominate your opponent from this position. Although my core art is karate, spending years developing my clinch game has only allowed me to implement my karate techniques more effectively. As a young man, I studied the Japanese art of Sumo, which provided me with a sturdy clinch base and gave me the body-to-body sensitivity needed to execute takedowns, throws, and off-balancing techniques. To compliment my Sumo background and further develop my clinch game, I worked extensively on my wrestling techniques. I trained to thwart a broad assortment of takedowns, as well as execute techniques that would allow me to haul my opponent to the mat. Always on a quest for knowledge, I then studied abroad in Thailand to master striking from the Muay Thai clinch.

In this section, I offer the clinching techniques that have worked best for me over the years in the MMA arena. Like all of the moves that I demonstrate, the clinching technique you employ should be based upon your opponent's movements and reactions. In other words, you want to use his energy to your advantage. For example, if your opponent drives forward while in the clinch, you can use his aggression to cast him off balance, which in turn allows you to land strikes or takedowns. If he attempts to pull away from you while tied up in the clinch, there is a different group of off-balancing techniques that allow you to achieve the same goal. And if he plays a more defensive game and waits for you to make a move, there is yet another group of techniques that allow you to force him to move in a certain direction. Once accomplished,

you can again use his energy to off-balance him and employ an attack. A lot of fighters have trouble in the clinch because they try to force a certain technique or resist their opponent's momentum, both of which burn precious energy and make you vulnerable to attack. In order to be a dangerous clinch fighter, you must develop body-to-body sensitivity and choose your techniques based upon the energy your opponent provides you.

3-1: Muay Thai Clinch

The Muay Thai clinch is designed for off-balancing your opponent and then landing devastating knee strikes to his body and head, but to be effective from this position, there are a few guidelines you must follow. First, position your arms to the inside of your opponent's arms. This is mandatory with the Muay Thai clinch, which involves cupping both of your hands around the back of your opponent's head, as well as with the head and arm clinch, which is where you wrap one hand around the back of his head and your other hand around the inside of his biceps. If you allow your opponent to pummel his arms to the inside of your arms, you will have lost your dominant position, making it impossible to execute the attacks demonstrated in this section. Second, use your control to shatter your opponent's base and balance by pulling his head downward. If you allow him to pull his head up and posture, he will reestablish his base and be in a much better position to defend against your attacks. Third, always execute your attack the instant you secure your dominant control. The goal is to break his stance, force him off balance, and then bombard him with knee strikes before he has a chance to defend against your position. Lastly, always use your opponent's energy to your advantage. If he moves forward, step to the side and pull him in the same direction he is traveling to disrupt his balance. If he retreats, follow him backward while throwing knees to his body and head. If he manages to execute an effective counter against your control, do not wait for him to escape— use the energy he feeds you to transition into another dominant clinch position. As long as you adhere to these guidelines, you will continuously off-balance your opponent in the Muay Thai clinch, creating openings to land devastating knee strikes.

3-2: Attacks from Neutral Clinch

When you are tied up in the clinch with your opponent, and you both have one overhook and one underhook, it is a neutral position because you both have the same offensive and defensive options. In this section, I demonstrate a number of Sumo and wrestling techniques that allow you to get the upper hand on your opponent. The goal with these moves is to use a combination of pushing and pulling movements to create a weakness in your opponent's base, and then exploit that weakness by executing a throw, trip, or takedown. When performed properly, all the techniques demonstrated in this section are low-risk, high-percentage moves that require minimal energy. Although securing a dominant hold such as the Muay Thai clinch is optimal, if your opponent is a good clinch player, chances are you will be spending an ample amount of time tied up in the neutral clinch. If you aren't a master at turning the tables in your favor, you could have a very long and exhausting battle in front of you.

3-3: Clinch Defense

In this section I demonstrate how to escape the two most dangerous clinch positions—the Muay Thai clinch and the double underhook bodylock. It's obviously better to avoid getting caught in these positions all together, but you always have to be prepared for the worst. If your opponent manages to cup his hands around the back of your head, you must escape the position before he can begin landing brutal knees to your body. And if he manages to pummel his arms underneath your arms and lock his hands together behind your back, you must escape before he can heft you off your feet and slam you to the mat. With each of

the escapes I offer, quickness is the key to success. The more time you give your opponent to secure his control, the less chance you have of pulling off a successful escape.

MUAY THAI CLINCH

SECURING THE MUAY THAI CLINCH

In this sequence I demonstrate one of several ways to control your opponent's head in the Muay Thai clinch. To obtain this particular control, reach both of your arms to the inside of your opponent's arms, grip your hands together around the back of his neck, and then use your grip to pull his head downward. To prevent your opponent from breaking your control by driving into you for the takedown, it is very important to position your elbows in front of his shoulders. Once you have hindered his movement and broken his posture, you are in an excellent position to begin throwing devastating knee strikes to his body and head. Later in this section I show other methods for controlling your opponent's head in the Muay Thai clinch, as well as more advanced techniques, but it is very important to have a strong grasp on the basics before progressing.

Chinzo and I are in a standard fighting stance with our left leg forward.

To assume control of Chinzo's head, I step my left foot forward, place my left forearm against the crevice on the right side of his neck, and reach my right hand to the inside of his left arm.

Keeping my elbows positioned in front of Chinzo's shoulders, I clamp both of my arms around the sides of his neck. Notice that my right thumb and wrist is flush with the back of his head.

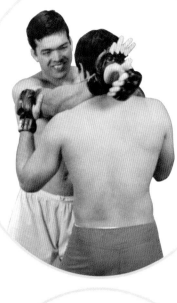

I grip my hands together around the back of Chinzo's head. It's important to note the placement of my grip. I position my hands underneath my opponent's skull in the small gap between his neck muscles and occipital bone.

With my grip intact, I pull down on Chinzo's head and break his posture—forcing his head down into my left shoulder. Note if your right palm is facing away from you then pull him down and toward your left shoulder as shown here. If you were to reverse your grip so that your left thumb is flush with his skull then you would pull his head down into your right shoulder.

STRAIGHT KNEE FROM MUAY THAI CLINCH

Once you've secured the Muay Thai clinch, throwing knee strikes to your opponent's body and head is an excellent option. There are a broad assortment of knee strikes at your disposal, but the straight knee is one of the most effective and destructive from the basic Thai clinch position. To execute this strike, pull your opponent's head down as you elevate your rear knee into his body or head. By pulling down on his head you not only break his stance, which makes it difficult for him to defend against your strike, but you also add considerable power to the knee. Although I only throw one knee in the sequence below, it is important to note that as long as you can keep your opponent's posture broken, you can continue to throw knee strike after knee strike. When I fought David Heath in the UFC, I managed to land seven knee strikes before he was able to free his head and escape the position.

Technical Note: In this sequence I have chosen to use a hand-over-hand grip to pull my opponent's head downward, but it's important to note that you can also use the grip demonstrated in the previous sequence to accomplish the same goal. As long as your elbows are positioned in front of your opponent's shoulders, the grip you use is a matter of choice.

I've secured the Muay Thai clinch on Chinzo. It is important to notice my grip. I have my left hand wrapped around the back of his neck and my right hand is cupped over the top of my left hand. It is also important to notice how I have pulled Chinzo's head down to break his posture. From here, I am in a perfect position to attack with a straight knee.

I pull Chinzo's head down and toward my right side using both of my arms. At the same time, I throw a straight knee toward his midsection.

Here I do several things at once. I lean my upper body slightly back, curl my right heel toward my right buttock, thrust my hips forward, and drive my right knee into Chinzo's midsection. To increase the power of the strike, I pull his head down in the direction of the knee. It's important to note that you also have the option of throwing the knee strike to your opponent's face. Although I end the sequence here with one knee strike, I will continue my assault by stringing together more knees or by off-balancing my opponent using the next technique in this section.

OFF-BALANCE TO KNEE STRIKE

When you are up against an opponent with a strong neck, it can sometimes be difficult to shatter his base by pulling his head downward. Instead of trying to fight his resistance with muscle, ripping him off balance using the technique demonstrated below is an excellent option. However, it is important not to get greedy. If you look at the photos below, you'll notice that I pull my opponent off balance, land a single knee strike, and then pull him in the opposite direction to prevent him from reestablishing his base. As long as you keep your opponent's base destroyed by pulling him from one side to the other, you will have numerous openings to attack. One of the most important components of this technique is maintaining a solid grip. If you focus too intently on your side-to-side movement and allow your grip to loosen, your opponent will most likely escape the position.

I've secured the Muay Thai clinch on Chinzo.

I step my right foot forward and to the outside of Chinzo's left leg. At the same time, I use my control to pull his head down and toward my left side.

3

Still pulling down on Chinzo's head, I turn my body in a counterclockwise direction, pivot on my right foot, and slide my left foot back.

4

I plant my left foot on the mat and prepare to unleash a knee to Chinzo's face.

5

Capitalizing on Chinzo's compromised position, I drive my left knee up into his face.

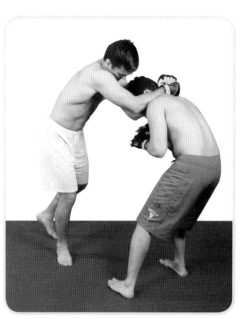

6

I return my left foot to its original position in my stance.

7

Chinzo attempts to counterbalance his weight and posture up. Before he can reestablish his base, I step my left foot forward and begin pulling him toward my right side. By switching my direction in this manner, I effectively use Chinzo's energy to my advantage.

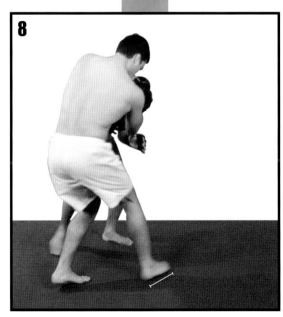

8

Still pulling down on Chinzo's head, I pivot on my left foot and start rotating my body in a clockwise direction.

9

Continuing with my previous movements, I slide my right foot back.

10

Keeping my grip tight on Chinzo's head, I plant my right foot on the mat and prepare to unleash another knee strike.

11

Still pulling down on Chinzo's head, I throw a straight knee to his midsection.

COUNTER CROSS-FACE WITH ARM DRAG TO KNEE

A lot of times when you secure the Muay Thai clinch your opponent will defend by driving his arm into your throat and pushing your head away from his body—a technique commonly referred to as the cross face. This creates separation, significantly weakens your grip on his head, and makes it difficult to land clean with a knee strike. In such a scenario, an excellent way to keep your offense going is to release the Muay Thai clinch and force his cross face arm to the outside of your body as demonstrated below. Although this puts you in an entirely different clinch position, it creates an opening to land a devastating knee strike to your opponent's face. Remember, you always have to base your attacks on your opponent's defense. If he counters your Muay Thai clinch, use the energy he feeds you to transition to another dominant clinch position.

I've secured the Muay Thai clinch on Chinzo. In an attempt to break my lock on his head, he drives his left arm into my chin and starts pushing my head away from his body.

To stifle Chinzo's escape attempt, I throw a right knee to his abdomen.

Here I do several things at once. I return my right foot to the mat, release my left grip on Chinzo's head, and grab the top of his left wrist with my left hand. At the same time, I cup my right hand around the back of his head and push his head down and away from my body.

I throw Chinzo's left arm downward and toward my right side using my left hand. As his arm swings across my body, I hook my right hand around the crook of his left elbow.

I redirect Chinzo's arm to the outside of my body with my right hand. At the same time, I wrap my left hand around the back of his head.

Having created a clear opening to attack with my previous actions, I extend my left arm into Chinzo's head and drive my left knee upward into his face.

HEAD AND ARM CONTROL TO SIDE KNEE

In this sequence I demonstrate how to establish head and arm control, as well as how to use your control to land a knee strike to your opponent's body. Head and arm control is different than the Muay Thai clinch in that instead of wrapping both of your hands around the back of your opponent's head, you wrap one hand around the back of his head and hook your other hand around the inside of his biceps. Although establishing head and arm control makes it harder to pull your opponent's head downward, it allows you to elevate one of his arms, creating a pathway to land either a straight knee to his abdomen or a side knee to his rib cage.

Chinzo and I are in a standard fighting stance with our left foot forward.

Chinzo advances forward in an attempt to tie me up in the clinch. As he closes the distance, I reach my left hand to the right side of his head and position my right arm to the inside of his left arm.

I wrap my left hand around the back of Chinzo's head, cup my right hand around the inside of his left biceps, and then flare my right elbow upward. Notice how this last action forces his arm up and opens the left side of his body to attack.

Keeping my right hand hooked tight around the inside of Chinzo's left arm, I pull down on his head with my left hand, start rotating my hips in a counterclockwise direction, and launch a right side knee toward the left side of his body.

Still pulling down on Chinzo's head as I rotate my hips, I lean my upper body slightly back and drive my right knee laterally into his left side.

CROSS KNEE BUMP FROM HEAD AND ARM CONTROL

In this sequence I demonstrate a highly effective off-balancing technique that can be utilized from head and arm control. Just as in the last sequence, I begin by securing the head and arm position, using my control to elevate my opponent's arm, and then landing a knee strike to his body. With my opponent thinking that I will remain stationary and attack, I circle around to the outside of his body immediately after landing my first knee strike. As I make this transition, I use my upper body control to pull him in the same direction. Although this will oftentimes off-balance my opponent, I don't rely on the turn alone. To help shatter his base, I drive my far knee into his lead leg, forcing it out from underneath him. The combination of these actions destroys my opponent's balance and causes him to collapse to the mat, giving me numerous attack options.

I've secured inside control on Chinzo's head and arm, giving me control over his upper body.

To set up my attack, I pull down on Chinzo's head with my left hand, rotate my hips in a counterclockwise direction, and lift my right knee toward his midsection. At the same time, I flare my right elbow skyward, exposing the left side of his body to attack.

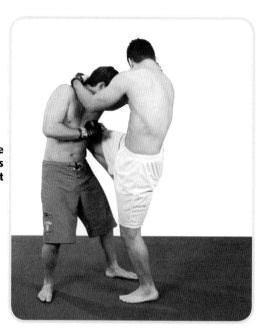

Still rotating my hips in a counterclockwise direction and pulling down on Chinzo's head, I drive my right kneecap into his left side.

I return my right foot to its original position in my stance.

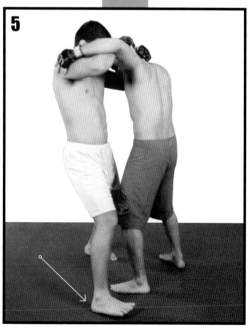

Having stunned Chinzo with the side knee, I step my right foot to the outside of his left foot. At the same time, I elevate my right arm to force his left arm upward and pull down on his head using my left arm.

6

Here I do several things at once. I pull down on Chinzo's head with my left hand while lifting his left arm skyward—like turning a big wheel. At the same time, I drive my left knee into the inside of his left thigh. It's important to note that the step, cross knee bump, and pull are all executed simultaneously. If you break up the sequence, then your opponent will adjust his stance and defend against your attack. At first this may seem awkward because you are pulling in the opposite direction of the knee bump. For that reason, it's imperative that you spend an ample amount of time drilling this technique in the gym before implementing it in a fight.

7

Chinzo is knocked off balance as a result of my previous actions.

8

Having kneed Chinzo's left leg out from underneath him, I step my left foot to the mat.

9

Still pulling on Chinzo's head to keep him off balance, I step my right leg back and square my hips with his head.

10

I reposition my left hand on the back of Chinzo's head and drive a right knee into his face. It's important to note that if you are fighting in an MMA-sanctioned event in America and your opponent has three points of control on the ground, then you will have to direct the knee to his body.

COUNTER BODYLOCK WITH UNDERHOOK TO REVERSE COLLAR TIE

When you are working to establish a dominant clinch position, your opponent will sometimes attempt to wrap his arms around your waist and secure a bodylock. This is especially true when your opponent is an experienced wrestler. If you allow him to achieve his goal, he gains the ability to pull your hips into his body, which not only nullifies your knee strikes, but also provides him with a number of attack options. In the sequence below, I demonstrate how to use this common counter to your advantage by establishing an underhook, transitioning to a reverse collar tie, and then landing knee strikes to your opponent's abdomen or face.

Chinzo and I are in standard fighting stances with our left leg forward.

In an attempt to secure a bodylock, Chinzo drops his level and shoots forward into my comfort zone. As he reaches for my waist, I pummel my right hand to the inside of his left arm and wrap my left hand around the right side of his head.

As I pummel my right hand to the inside of Chinzo's left arm, I wrap my left hand around the back of his head, positioning my elbow in front of his shoulder. With this action, I effectively halt his forward progression and nullify his bodylock. Next, I pull down on his head using my left hand and wrap my right arm around the back of his left shoulder.

I maneuver my left arm to the left side of Chinzo's head and step my right foot forward and to the outside of his left foot.

I slide my left foot back and establish a dominant angle of attack. To further break Chinzo's base, I push down on his head with my left arm and crank down on his left shoulder with my right underhook.

Having broken Chinzo's base and created an opening to attack, I drive a left straight knee into his face.

INSIDE HAND TRAP TO OVER-THE-TOP ELBOW

In this sequence I demonstrate how to break your opponent's guard using a hand trap, and then use that opening to land an over-the-top elbow strike to his face. While it can sometimes be difficult to knock your opponent out with an over-the-top elbow due to its downward trajectory, landing a clean blow will often open a cut and momentarily discombobulate your opponent, giving you an opportunity to follow up with another attack. Although there are numerous follow-up attacks that you can employ, over the next several pages I've included the two options that I have found to be the most effective. In sequence A, I demonstrate how to follow up with a ruthless uppercut elbow, and in sequence B I demonstrate how to pummel your arm to the inside of your opponent's arm and secure an underhook.

I'm squared off with Chinzo in a standard fighting stance.

To break Chinzo's guard, I hook my left hand around the inside of his left hand and then pull his arm down.

Having created an opening to attack with my previous actions, I draw my left arm back into my stance, begin rotating my hips in a counterclockwise direction, and elevate my right elbow. To protect the left side of my face from counterstrikes, I've elevated my left arm.

As I rotate my body, I come up onto the ball of my rear foot and turn my hand over so that my thumb is pointing toward the mat. Notice how this last action forces my elbow skyward.

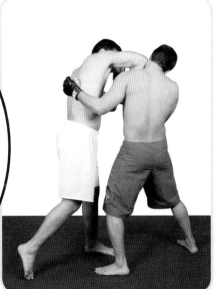

Still rotating my body in a counterclockwise direction, I throw my elbow along a downward arc and into the left side of Chinzo's face. To protect my face from counterstrikes, I've kept my left hand up at eye level.

SEQUENCE A: OVER-THE-TOP ELBOW TO UPPERCUT ELBOW

In this sequence I demonstrate how to transition from an over-the-top elbow directly into an uppercut elbow. If you look at the photos, you'll notice that by following through with the over-the-top elbow, my upper body turns toward the ground. Instead of returning to my stance and then throwing the uppercut elbow, I throw it as I straighten my body. Not only does this allow me to flow from one strike to the next, but it also dramatically increases power in the uppercut elbow.

I've landed a rear over-the-top elbow to the left side of Chinzo's jaw.

As I pull my right arm back into my stance, I rotate my hips in a clockwise direction and elevate my left elbow toward Chinzo's chin.

I drive the tip of my left elbow upward into Chinzo's chin.

SEQUENCE B: OVER-THE-TOP ELBOW TO BODYLOCK COUNTER

In this sequence I stun my opponent with an over-the-top elbow, but instead of holding his ground as he did in the previous sequence, he immediately attempts to wrap his arms around my waist to hinder me from landing more strikes. To prevent him from securing a bodylock, I follow through with my over-the-top elbow, swim my striking arm to the inside of his left arm to secure an underhook, and then reposition my body off to his side. The combination of these actions not only allows me to defend against his bodylock, but it also sets me up to throw devastating knee strikes to his body or head.

I've landed a rear over-the-top elbow to the left side of Chinzo's jaw.

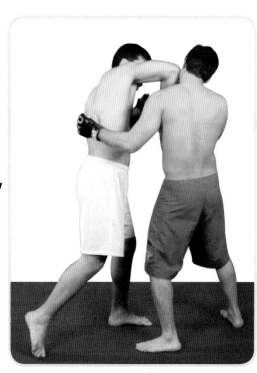

I follow through with the right elbow and maneuver my right arm to the inside of Chinzo's left arm. At the same time, I reach my left arm toward the left side of his head.

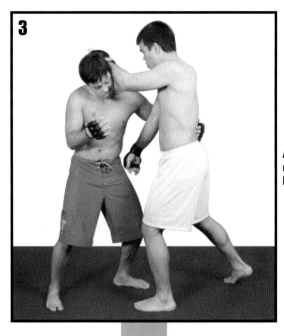

As I swing my right arm to the outside of my body, I jam my left forearm into the left side of Chinzo's head.

I pull Chinzo's head down with my left hand and hook my right hand around the back of his left shoulder.

In order to set up a left knee, I have to re-verse the positioning of my feet. To begin this process, I slide my left foot back.

6

As my left foot touches down, I slide my right foot forward and prepare to unleash a knee to Chinzo's face.

7

Still pushing Chinzo's head away from my body with my left hand and pulling down on his left shoulder with my right hand, I drive my left knee up into his face.

INSIDE KNEE BLOCK

The inside knee block is a common sumo wrestling technique that translates well to MMA. This particular move works best when your opponent drives his weight forward from the neutral clinch. For example, if you are tied up with your opponent in the center of the octagon and he tries to push you up against the cage, transitioning to the inside knee block to knock him off balance or throw him to the mat is an excellent option. If you look at the photos below, you'll notice that I circle toward my opponent's left side, hook my right hand to the inside of his left leg, and then turn my body in the direction of my step. The combination of these actions creates a hole for my opponent's weight to fall into, and with my hand preventing him from counterbalancing his weight, he plummets straight to the mat. The nice part about this technique is it gives you multiple attack options. For instance, if you want to keep the fight standing, you can remain on your feet and begin plotting your next attack, which is what I demonstrate below. If your goal is to take the fight to the mat, you can follow your opponent to the ground and begin your assault from the top position. If you execute the inside knee block and your opponent manages to stay on his feet, chances are his base and balance will be compromised, allowing you to immediately set up another attack.

I'm in a neutral clinch position with Chinzo. I've got an overhook and an underhook, and he has an overhook and an underhook.

To get my offense going, I circle my body toward Chinzo's left side, hook my right hand to the inside of his left knee so that the knuckles of my fist are flush with his thigh, and pull down on his right lat using my left hand.

3

Still rotating my body in a counterclockwise direction and pulling down on Chinzo's right lat using my left hand, I elevate my right hand into his left leg.

4

As a result of my previous actions, Chinzo loses his balance and topples toward the mat.

5

Chinzo collapses to the mat. It is important to note that you can either drop down on top of your opponent or remain standing as I do here. The option you choose should be based upon your goals in the fight.

OUTSIDE LEG TRIP OPTION 1

The outside leg trip is one of my favorite wrestling takedowns to execute when tied up in the neutral over-under clinch. There are two versions of this takedown that I utilize. The first option, which I demonstrate below, works the best when your opponent moves backward or tries to pull away from the clinch. The second option, which I demonstrate in the next sequence, works the best when he drives his weight forward and pushes into you. Like all countering techniques that have multiple versions, the option you choose should be based upon the energy of your opponent.

I'm tied up with Chinzo in the neutral clinch position.

To secure control over Chinzo's upper body, I grip my hands together in the small of his back.

Now that I have secured a bodylock, I step my left leg deep behind Chinzo's right leg, closing off all space between our bodies. This step is very important. If you take a shallow step or give up space, your opponent will most likely defend against the attack.

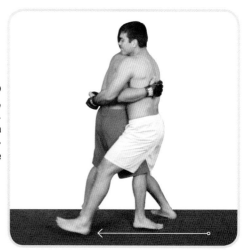

I plant my left foot on the mat directly behind Chinzo's left heel. Notice how all space has been closed off between our bodies. Next, I start corkscrewing my body in a counterclockwise direction and pull his upper body toward my left side. It's important to note how I clamp down on his right arm with my left arm, trapping it to my side.

Still corkscrewing my body in a counterclockwise direction, I pull Chinzo over my left leg. Because my leg is serving as a barrier, he sits over my left thigh and starts to collapse toward the mat.

I land on my left side and throw Chinzo to the mat.

Using my counterclockwise rotation to my advantage, I throw my right leg over my left leg and secure top control. With this technique, it is imperative that you stay tight to your opponent's body and execute all the steps in one fluid motion. If you allow space or hesitate between steps, your opponent will most likely defend against your attack.

KNEE TO OUTSIDE LEG TRIP OPTION 2

In this sequence I demonstrate another version of the outside leg trip. Unlike the previous technique, which works best when your opponent drives his weight away from you, this technique works best when your opponent pushes his weight into you. If you look at the photos below, you'll notice that as my opponent steps forward, I quickly shuffle my feet and position my leg to the outside of his lead leg. The instant he transfers his weight onto his lead leg, I fall backward while corkscrewing my body, pulling him over my leg and forcing him to collapse to the mat. With both this version and the previous one, the key is to stay tight to your opponent and execute all of the steps in one fluid motion.

I'm tied up with Chinzo in the neutral clinch.

I throw a left straight knee to Chinzo's abdomen to get my offense going.

As I bring my leg back down to the mat, Chinzo steps forward with his right foot and pushes into me. To capitalize on his forward energy, I wrap my left arm around his right arm and cinch down on his underhook with my overhook.

As Chinzo's right foot touches down, I step my left leg deep to the outside of his right leg and begin falling toward my left side. It's important to notice that I've kept my upper body clinch tight and closed off all space between our bodies using my hips.

Capitalizing on Chinzo's forward energy, I fall toward my left side, causing him to lose his balance and trip over my left leg. Note how I pull him toward my left with my left overhook while driving my right underhook into his left armpit.

6

As I land on my left side, I immediately begin rolling over my left shoulder.

7

I roll toward my stomach and throw my right leg over my left leg.

8

I plant my right knee on the mat next to Chinzo's right hip. From here, I will immediately start attacking from the side control position.

KNEE-BLOCK TAKEDOWN

If you've been reading through this section sequentially, then you already know how to counter your opponent's energy when he is pushing into you as well as how to counter his energy when he is pulling away from you. Now I will show you how to set up a takedown when your opponent is doing nothing and simply stalling in the position. To set up this particular technique, you want to step your rear leg to the outside of his lead foot while pulling on his far lat with your underhook. In order to maintain his balance, he will be forced to step his foot in the direction of your turn. To capitalize on his forward step, cup the hand of your overhook arm around the outside of his knee while driving your underhook upward into his armpit. With his upper body being pushed over his trapped leg, he will lose his balance and collapse to his back. It's important to note that your success with this takedown is dependent on your ability to time and anticipate your opponent's forced step. If your timing is off, then your window of opportunity will close and you will be back to square one.

I'm tied up with Chinzo in the neutral clinch.

In order to set up my attack, I first have to force Chinzo to turn and step his rear foot forward. To begin this process, I step my left leg to the outside of his right leg, pull on his left lat with my right hand, and turn my body in a clockwise direction. Notice how these actions cause my opponent to turn with me.

Still pulling on Chinzo's left lat with my right underhook and rotating my body in a clockwise direction, I pivot on my left foot and slide my right foot back. The combination of these actions forces my opponent to turn a hundred eighty degrees from his original position.

The moment Chinzo's left foot touches down, I shift my weight onto my right leg, drive my right foot off the mat, step my left foot to the outside of his right leg, drop my left shoulder toward the mat, and drive my right underhook upward into his left armpit.

Still extending my right arm upward into Chinzo's left armpit, I place my left hand on the outside of his right knee to prevent him from stepping and regaining his balance.

I drive Chinzo's upper body over his trapped leg, causing him to collapse toward the mat.

Chinzo collapses to his back. From here, I can follow him to the ground to assume top control or remain standing and execute my attack from the downed guard position.

INSIDE LEG TRIP

In the previous sequence I showed you how to force your opponent into stepping his rear foot forward to set up a knee-block takedown. In this sequence, I utilize the same setup, but instead of attacking the foot in motion as I did in the previous sequence, I attack his grounded leg with an inside leg trip. It's important to note that unlike the previous technique, which gives you the option of going to the ground or to remain in the standing position, this technique requires you to follow your opponent to the mat. If your goal is to keep the fight standing, the knee-block takedown is a much better option. However, if your goal is to impose your will on the ground, then the inside leg trip is your best bet because not only do you land in your opponent's half guard, but you are in a perfect position from which to pass into side control.

I'm tied up with Chinzo in the neutral clinch.

In order to set up my attack, I have to force Chinzo to turn and step his rear foot forward. To begin this process, I step my left leg to the outside of his right leg while pulling on his left lat with my right hand.

As a result of my previous actions, Chinzo is forced into a clockwise turn, causing him to step his left foot forward.

The moment Chinzo's left foot touches down, I drive off the mat using my left foot, drop my elevation, and wrap my right leg around the inside of his right leg.

I hook my right leg around the back of Chinzo's right leg.

6

I drop my weight over Chinzo's right leg, causing it to hyperextend.

7

Chinzo collapses to his back.

8

As Chinzo rolls to his back, I slide my left leg up the mat and collapse my chest over his hips, pinning his back to the mat. From here, I will work to pass his half guard to a more dominant position such as side control or mount.

DRAG-DOWN OFF OVER-UNDER CLINCH

In this sequence I demonstrate how to utilize the drag-down when tied up with your opponent in the over-under clinch. Unlike the previous two techniques, which required a forced movement, this technique is best employed when your opponent drives into you. The instant you feel his weight press forward, back away to create space between your bodies and then quickly circle around to his side. This creates a hole for him to fall into and allows you to drag him down to the mat as demonstrated below.

I'm tied up with Chinzo in the neutral clinch. Note how he is pushing forward and dropping his weight over my right underhook. To capitalize on his energy, I will create space between us by circling to the outside of his body.

To create space, I posture up, hook the webbing of my left hand around the crook of Chinzo's right arm, and then push down on his underhook.

Having created space with my previous actions, I hook my right hand around the back of Chinzo's left shoulder. It's important to note that by stripping him of his right underhook, I prevent him from following me as I circle around to the side of his body. Normally, when you drive your weight into your opponent and create separation as demonstrated here, he will resist with more forward pressure of his own, which only helps with the application of this technique.

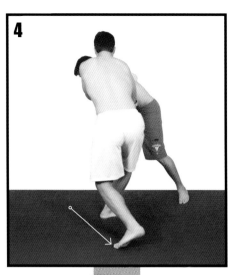

Pivoting on my right foot, I rotate my body in a counterclockwise direction and slide my left foot back. At the same time, I place my left hand over my right hand and apply downward pressure to the back of Chinzo's left shoulder.

Still circling around to Chinzo's left side and applying downward pressure on his left shoulder using both of my hands, I break his posture and force his head toward the mat. Although this can sometimes be difficult to manage, by using the momentum of my counterclockwise turn in combination with his forward energy, it is much easier to complete my goal.

Keeping my right arm hooked around the back of Chinzo's left arm, I reach my left hand over the back of his head.

I wrap my left arm around the right side of Chinzo's neck and collapse my chest over the back of his left shoulder.

8

I grip my hands together and then pull Chinzo's head into me. It's important to mention that I'm pressing my weight through my left shoulder into his upper back. This puts downward pressure on his upper body and makes it difficult for him to scramble out of the position or work for a takedown.

9

As Chinzo falls to all fours due to my previous actions, I immediately begin circling toward his left side.

10

Continuing to circle my body in a counterclockwise direction, I wrap my right arm around Chinzo's right side, post up on my left leg, and then cock my left hand back. It's important to notice how I've closed off all space between our bodies. It's also important to note that I am driving all of my weight into his back. The combination of these actions prevents him from rolling forward over his left shoulder and pulling me into guard or escaping the position by standing up. From here you can start throwing punches to your opponent's face, secure back control and work for a choke, or return to the standing position.

DOUBLE UNDERHOOK KNEE-LIFT TAKEDOWN

In this sequence I demonstrate one of the most effective takedowns that you can utilize when you secure the double under-hook bodylock position. A part of what makes this particular move so effective is its simplicity. Most bodylock takedowns require you to circle around to your opponent's back before executing the takedown. Although this approach works, it makes you vulnerable to counterattacks, such as the kimura submission and the headlock throw. A much better option is to lift your opponent into the air from the front bodylock position and then slam him to the mat. This decreases your risk of getting countered, which in turn increases your chances of executing a successful takedown.

I've secured a double underhook bodylock on Chinzo.

Keeping my arms locked tight around Chinzo's body, I step my left foot forward and close off all space between our bodies.

In one fluid motion, I thrust my hips forward and lift Chinzo up off the mat. As I heft him up, I elevate my right knee into his crotch to raise him even higher off the mat. It's important to note that I'm not kneeing him in the groin; I'm using my leg to help generate upward momentum and increase the velocity of my lift.

As Chinzo reaches peak elevation, I release my grip, dip my left shoulder toward the mat, hook my left hand around the outside of his right leg, and drive my right underhook into his left side.

Still driving my underhook into Chinzo's left side, I pull his right leg underneath me with my left hand and throw him toward the mat.

Unable to plant his right leg to the mat to stop his fall, Chinzo plummets to his back. From here, I will immediately capitalize on his stunned state with an attack.

SHOULDER SHRUG ESCAPE FROM MUAY THAI CLINCH

If your opponent wraps his arms around your head to secure the Muay Thai clinch, executing the shoulder shrug escape is an excellent way to turn the tables in your favor. When performed properly, you not only break your opponent's lock on your head and escape the position, but you also create an opening to attack. The key is to execute the escape the moment your opponent gains control of your head. If you hesitate for a split second, your opponent will most likely pull your head down, making this particular escape difficult to manage.

Chinzo has gained control of my head by securing the Muay Thai clinch. Before he can execute an attack from the position, I posture up and maneuver my right hand to the inside of his left arm.

I wrap my left hand around the back of Chinzo's head, use that control to pull him toward my left, and drive my left shoulder upward into his right elbow. At the same time, I wedge my right forearm into the crook of his left elbow and push his arm outward.

Still driving my left shoulder into Chinzo's right arm and pulling on his head with my left hand, I draw my right shoulder back and rotate my body in a clockwise direction. The combination of these actions forces his right arm off my head.

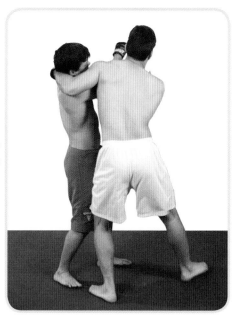

Now that I have broken Chinzo's lock on my head, I latch on to his right arm with my right hand.

To create an opening and set up a knee strike, I pull on Chinzo's right arm with my right hand and slide my right foot back.

Having created an opening to Chinzo's body, I apply downward pressure on his head with my left hand and throw a right knee to his midsection.

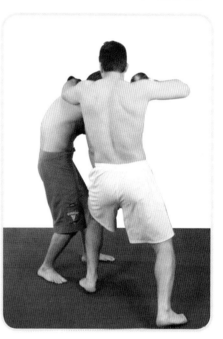

I return to my stance and prepare to follow up my assault with a right elbow.

I land a right elbow to the right side of Chinzo's head.

OUTSIDE LEG TRIP (COUNTER DOUBLE UNDERHOOKS)

When your opponent manages to pummel both of his arms underneath your arms and secure a double underhook body-lock, there is a good chance that he will attempt to clasp his hands together behind your back, pull your body into his, and then use his control to throw you to the mat. To prevent such an outcome, the instant he secures the bodylock, create distance between your bodies by wrapping your arms over his arms and sprawling your hips back. With his attack options limited, it gives you a window of opportunity to employ the outside leg trip demonstrated in the sequence below. The key to being successful with this technique is keeping your overhooks locked tight over your opponent's arms. If you relax your grip, he will be able to free his arms from your grasp and avoid the takedown.

1

Chinzo has gained control of my body by secur-ing a double underhook bodylock. To weaken his hold, I've wrapped both of my arms around the outside of his arms.

2

To prevent Chinzo from hauling me to the mat, I have to create separation between our bod-ies. I accomplish this by cinching down on his underhooks with my overhooks and stepping my left leg back. Also notice how I sink my hips back and drop my weight down. This adds additional pressure to my opponent's hold, making it extremely difficult for him to close the distance and pull my body into his.

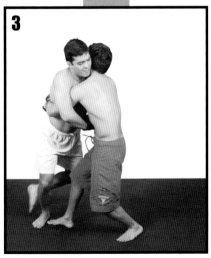

3

In an attempt to close the distance, Chinzo steps his right foot forward. To capitalize on this, I shuffle my feet and maneuver my left leg to the outside of his right leg.

I plant my left foot on the mat behind Chinzo's right leg.

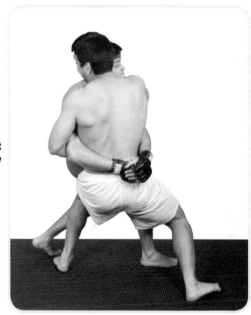

Keeping both of my arms locked tight around Chinzo's arms, I fall toward my left and pull him over my left leg.

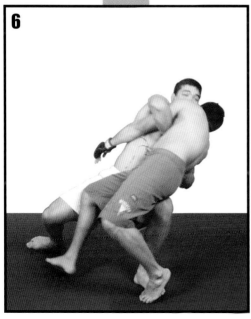

As I fall to my left side, Chinzo trips over my left leg and plummets toward the mat.

7

As I hit the mat, I turn into Chinzo to secure top control

8

I roll toward my belly and step my right leg over my left leg. From here, I will immediately get my offense going from side control.

PART FOUR
ATTACKING THE GUARD

Whether you trip your opponent to the mat with a foot sweep, knock him down with a strike, or haul him to the ground with a takedown, chances are you will get wrapped up in between his legs in either his full, open, or half guard. If you don't know how to fight from your opponent's guard, there is a good chance that he will climb to his feet or execute a sweep or submission.

To prevent these outcomes, it is imperative that you remain on the offensive by throwing strikes and working to pass his legs and achieve a more dominant position such as side control or the mount. To help you with this goal, I've provided a number of highly effective ground and pound combinations, as well as several passing techniques from the downed guard, closed guard, open guard, and half guard positions. While all of these positions are separated into individual sections, it's important to note that the techniques are all interconnected. For example, you can throw an over-the-top elbow to force your opponent's legs open from the closed guard, and then pass into his half guard. From the half guard, you can throw some more punches and then transition to a leglock or pass his guard into side control. Ultimately, the path you choose depends upon the situation and the openings that are available. The most important thing is that you remain on the offensive and use your strikes in conjuncture with your passing techniques to set up your attack. By blending the techniques presented in this chapter together, you not only shift your opponent's focus from an offensive mind-set to a defensive one, but you also make it difficult for him to defend against your attacks.

4-1: Attacking the Downed Guard

There are many ways you can end up standing in front of a downed opponent. You can knock him down with a strike, trip him to the mat with a foot sweep, or stand up and back out of his guard. Regardless of how you end up in this situation, it is important that you capitalize on your opponent's vulnerable position by immediately initiating an attack. Although there are many different tactics you can use, I personally like obtaining control of my opponent's feet to prevent him from standing up or pulling me into his guard, and then use that control to set up strikes such as the roundhouse kick or axe kick. If your goal is to keep the fight on the ground, as you will see, you can use these strikes to help pass your opponent's guard into a more dominant control position. With all of the attacks that I demonstrate, whether it is a strike or a pass, it is important that you maintain your posture. If you dip your head forward, you risk getting knocked out with an up-kick to the face.

4-2: Attacking the Full Guard

Getting stuck in your opponent's closed guard can be dangerous because he can use both of his arms and legs to attack your upper body. To reduce his attack options and open your offense, your first order of business should be to pin his back to the mat and posture up. Creating this space between your bodies not only decreases your vulnerability, but it also allows you to use your hips and the weight of your entire body to generate powerful downward strikes.

When you shut your opponent's offense down in

this fashion, he will often look to obtain another form of control. Quite often, he will grab on to your wrists to hinder you from throwing strikes, as well as to help him set up sweeps and submissions. This form of control is known as double wrist control, and although it can hinder you from attacking in a jiu-jitsu match, it does little to hinder your offense in MMA. In this section, I demonstrate how to free your hands from double wrist control and then deliver powerful punches and elbows. I also show how to use these strikes to help set up guard passing techniques.

4-3: Attacking the Half Guard

When in your opponent's half guard, you only have to battle half of his body, making it a much easier position to attack from than his full guard. With just one leg trapped between your opponent's legs, you have many options for striking, passing his guard into a more dominant position, or working for a submission such as a leglock. Regardless of the attack you employ, it is important to pay close attention to your positioning. Just as you would when attacking your opponent's full guard, you must keep his back pinned firmly to the mat. If you allow him to turn onto his side and secure an underhook, he can transition to your back or reverse the position by utilizing a sweep. Along these same lines, if you allow him to move his free leg to the inside of your body, he can create space between you and pull you into his full guard, which gives him a lot more control. To prevent these negative outcomes, it is important not to get so wrapped up with striking that you neglect your opponent's actions. If he starts to sit up or shrimp his hips, drop your weight over his trapped leg and collapse your chest over his torso. Once you flatten his back to the mat again, you can pop back up to a postured position and throw more strikes to his body and head. As long as you keep control at the top of your to-do list, several striking, passing, and submission opportunities will be available.

ROUND KICK

When you are standing over a downed opponent, he will often place his feet on your lead leg in an attempt to maintain distance between your bodies and prevent you from attacking. In such a scenario, a good option is to grab his inside leg, force it to the side, and then land a round kick to his exposed thigh. It is important to note that there are two methods for securing control of your opponent's leg. You can grab the outside of his foot, as demonstrated in sequence A, or you can grab the inside of his foot, as demonstrated in sequence B. Both methods are just as effective, and deciding which one to employ boils down to personal choice. The key with both techniques is keeping your head out of harm's way by maintaining posture and executing the grab and kick in one fluid motion.

SEQUENCE A: OUTSIDE GRAB TO LEG KICK

1) I'm standing in front of Chinzo, searching for an opening to attack. Notice how he's placed both of his feet on my lead leg in an attempt to maintain distance. 2) To create an opening to attack, I first have to clear Chinzo's feet off my left leg. To accomplish this, I reach down with my left hand and grab the outside of his left leg. 3) In one fluid motion, I rip Chinzo's left foot off of my lead leg and throw a right low kick underneath his left leg. 4) I land a right low kick to the outside of Chinzo's left leg.

SEQUENCE B: INSIDE GRAB TO LEG KICK

I'm standing in front of Chinzo, searching for an opening to attack. Notice how he's placed both of his feet on my lead leg in an attempt to maintain distance.

I grab the inside of Chinzo's left leg with my left hand.

To create an opening for the right low kick, I pull up on Chinzo's left foot.

As I pull Chinzo's left foot upward, I rotate my hips in a counter-clockwise direction and throw a right low kick to the outside of his left leg.

AXE KICK

When you are standing over a downed opponent who has strong defense, it can sometimes be difficult to gain control of his legs or sneak past his guard. In such a scenario, and excellent option is to employ an axe kick. It is a difficult strike to see coming, which makes it very hard for your opponent to defend against. Once you land the kick, you have a couple of options. You can step through your opponent's guard and land a hammer fist to his head, which is demonstrated in the next sequence, or retract your leg, reestablish your stance, and begin plotting your next attack.

1) I'm standing a few feet away from Chinzo, searching for an opening to attack. 2) I take a small outward step with my left foot and begin rotating my hips in a counterclockwise direction. 3) Still turning my hips in a counterclockwise direction, I shift my weight onto my left leg and swing my right leg toward the left side of my body. 4) Keeping my right leg straight and continuing to swing my right foot in counterclockwise direction, I draw my right knee toward my chest and elevate my foot toward the ceiling. 5) Having cleared Chinzo's guard, I drop my right leg straight down—using the momentum of my circular swing to my advantage—and drive the heel of my foot into his abdomen. It's important to notice how I keep my foot flexed upward. This ensures that my heel lands first as I bring my leg down.

STOMP KICK TO HAMMER FIST

In this sequence I demonstrate how to land a stomp kick to the face of a downed opponent, and then follow up with a hammer fist to the side of his head. If you look at the photos below, you'll notice that I begin the technique by gaining control of both of my opponent's legs. This is a critical step because it prevents him from blocking my strike by balling up, as well as from transitioning to a leglock as I step through his guard to land the hammer fist. It is important to note that stomping a downed opponent in the face has been banned in MMA competitions in the United States, but it is still legal in many fighting organizations overseas, including those in Japan and Brazil. If you fight exclusively in the United States, instead of stomping on your opponent's face, you'll want to drive your foot down into his abdomen.

1

I'm hovering over Chinzo, searching for an opening to attack. Notice how he's placed both of his feet on my lead leg in an attempt to maintain distance.

2

I reach down and grab the inside of Chinzo's ankles with both of my hands.

3

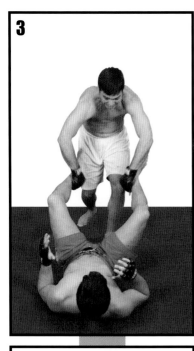

Having gained control of Chinzo's feet, I pull up on his ankles and separate his legs.

4

As I separate his legs, I draw my right knee toward my chest and step my right leg through his guard.

5

I stomp my right heel down into Chinzo's face. It is important to remember that if you are fighting in a competition in the United States, direct the heel strike to your opponent's solar plexus instead of his face.

Instead of pulling my right leg back into my stance, I plant my right foot on the mat on the left side of Chinzo's head.

Before Chinzo can regain his composure, I grab his right wrist using my left hand to limit his options. At the same time, I cock my right hand back and prepare to drop a hammer fist to his face.

I chop my right hand down and drive my fist into the right side of Chinzo's jaw.

FLYING PUNCH (CARTWHEEL PASS)

In this sequence I demonstrate how to cartwheel over the legs of a downed opponent, deliver a powerful punch to his face as your body sails through the air, and then land in the side control position. It's a highly effective technique, but even when you execute it correctly, sometimes your opponent will manage to sneak a leg in front of your body to prevent you from establishing side control. In such a scenario, you can stand back up and once again attempt the cartwheel pass or transition to the next guard passing technique demonstrated in this section.

Technical Note: **This is a dynamic move that requires commitment and agility. If you don't feel comfortable attempting the maneuver, executing one of the other techniques in this section as means of landing a strike or passing your opponent's guard is a much better option.**

I'm standing a few feet away from Chinzo, searching for an opening to attack.

Shifting a larger portion of my weight onto my left leg, I lean my upper body forward and reach my left hand toward Chinzo's chest. Timing is critical when executing this step. You have to act fast and commit. If you hesitate, your opponent will time your movement and throw an up-kick to your face.

I plant my left hand on Chinzo's chest, drive off the mat with my left foot, and then cartwheel through his guard. Using my left arm to keep me momentarily suspended in the air, I coil my left leg into my left buttock and bring my right fist down in the direction of his face.

With the momentum of the cartwheel carrying me forward, I land a heavy overhand right to the left side of Chinzo's jaw.

Having landed a hard punch to Chinzo's face, I begin descending toward the mat.

I plant my right knee on the mat to the left side of Chinzo's body. Notice that I've kept my right fist planted on his face. This not only prevents him from turning into me, but it also keeps me balanced as I drop toward the mat.

Although I've landed a hard overhand to Chinzo's face, I haven't quite cleared his legs. From here, I will use his stunned state to my advantage and quickly pass his guard into side control.

PASSING THE DOWNED GUARD

Standing above a downed opponent is an excellent way to land strikes, but with there still being a good deal of space between you, he has a decent chance of making a quick escape back to his feet. If you feel your grappling skills are better than his, sometimes your best option for maintaining a dominant position is to pass his guard and secure side control. This can be achieved using the cartwheel pass demonstrated in the previous sequence or by using the technique demonstrated below. To properly set up this technique, secure control of one of your opponent's feet, force it between your legs, and then drop down into his guard by falling to your knees. With your opponent's foot still trapped between your legs, he will have a very difficult time pulling you into his full guard, which limits his offensive options. To make your transition to side control, simply push down on the knee of his trapped leg, step your body over his leg, and then circle around to his side. Although it is a highly effective pass, it is important to assess your opponent's skill level before utilizing this technique. If his ground skills are better than yours, you'll be better off remaining standing and employing one of the striking techniques previously demonstrated. If your opponent is a jiu-jitsu black belt and your forte is striking, the last thing you want to do is willingly engage him in a grappling match.

Having gained control of Chinzo's left leg, I'm in a good position to start passing his guard.

To begin my attack, I pull Chinzo's left foot off my right leg using my right hand. At the same time, I reach down and grab the top of his right instep with my left hand and force his right heel toward his right buttock. Notice how I form my grip so that the webbing of my left hand is wrapped around the top of his right ankle. With this grip, I can effectively force his leg to bend. This prevents him from wrapping his leg around my body and pulling me into his full guard.

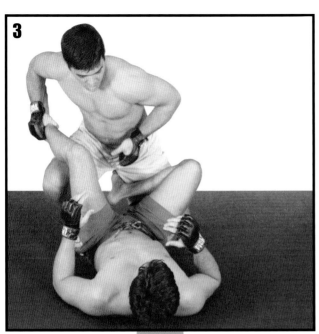

I slide my right foot underneath Chinzo's left buttock, press my weight forward, and drop my left knee toward the mat. At the same time, I drop my elevation, release my left grip on his right leg, and hook his right foot to the inside of my left leg. It's important that you execute this step as one seamless movement. If you hesitate or give space, your opponent will be able to nullify your attack by shifting his hips and creating a scramble.

Having trapped Chinzo's right leg underneath my body, I drop my butt to the mat and collapse my weight over his hips.

Keeping my weight distributed over Chinzo's body, I place my left hand on top of his right knee and hook my right arm underneath his left arm. By securing a right underhook on his left arm, I can effectively keep his shoulders pinned to the mat as I pass into side control. If you fail to secure a far-side underhook in this situation, not only will you fail in passing your opponent's guard, but you will give him the upper hand and most likely put yourself in a position of compromise.

6

Still pushing in on Chinzo's right knee using my left hand, I shift my weight onto my left knee and straighten my right leg.

7

Using the weight of my upper body to keep Chinzo's back pinned to the mat, I turn my hips in a clockwise direction and throw my right leg back.

8

Having cleared Chinzo's legs, I slide my left knee up to his right hip. This prevents him from sliding his right leg underneath me and pulling me back into his guard.

I maneuver my left arm to the left side of Chinzo's head.

To secure side control, I plant my left elbow on the mat, maneuver my right leg over my left leg, and fall to my left hip. From here, I will immediately get my offense going from side control.

FOOT LOCK

In this sequence I demonstrate how to apply a foot lock when you are standing over a downed opponent. It is important to mention that this technique is inherently risky. If each step isn't performed correctly, there is a good chance that you will wind up on your back with your opponent on top of you. For this reason, it is best to reserve this technique for the final seconds of a round. In the best case scenario, you slap on the submission and force your opponent to tap before the end of the round. If your opponent has an iron will, sometimes he will endure the pain until the clock runs out, but the submission will still cause significant damage to his foot, making it hard for him to continue in the next round. In the worst case scenario, you lose the submission and your opponent quickly climbs on top of you, but because it is the end of the round, he won't have time to capitalize on his dominant position. Although this isn't ideal, it still looks good on the judges' scorecards because you made an attempt to finish the fight.

Having secured control of Chinzo's legs, I'm in a good position to attack.

Using my right hand, I maneuver Chinzo's left foot toward the left side of my body.

As I force Chinzo's left leg across my body, I wrap my left arm around the inside of his left leg.

I drop my upper body toward the mat so that Chinzo's left instep is flush with my left armpit. It's important to notice how my left foot is positioned underneath his hips. This will allow me to close off all space between our bodies as I drop to the mat to secure the leglock.

Wrapping my left arm tight around Chinzo's left leg, I post my right hand on the mat, sit straight down to my right hip, hook my right leg around the outside of his left leg, and then position my right foot over his left hip. It's important to notice how I've closed off all space between our hips. If you give up space, your chances of pulling off the submission drop dramatically.

I drop to my right elbow and clamp my right leg tight around Chinzo's left leg. It's important to notice that I'm digging my right foot into his abdomen. This not only prevents him from sitting up into me to defend against the leglock, but it also positions my foot out of harm's way should he attempt to counter the submission with a leglock of his own. It is also important to notice that I'm driving the blade of my left wrist into the back of his left ankle.

To finish the foot lock, I pinch my knees together, corkscrew my shoulders in a clockwise direction, thrust my hips forward, and arc back. Note that I keep my right leg coiled tight around Chinzo's left leg and maintain a tight lock around his ankle with my left arm. Also notice how I'm on my side and looking in the direction of my turn. With these actions, I cause Chinzo severe pain and discomfort, forcing him to tap out in submission.

HAND TRAP TO ELBOW

A lot of times when you are kneeling in your opponent's closed guard, he will grab hold of your wrists to prevent you from striking. In the sequence below, I demonstrate how to break this control and land a powerful over-the-top elbow to your opponent's face. When studying the photos, pay close attention to how I break my opponent's grip on my right arm using my left hand, and then pin his arm to his chest as I deliver a right elbow. This pin not only prevents him from reforming his grip on my right wrist, but it also prevents him from elevating his arm and blocking my strike.

I'm in Chinzo's closed guard. In an attempt to nullify my strikes, he has latched on to both of my wrists.

In order to get my offense going, I first have to break Chinzo's grip on my wrist. To begin this process, I elevate my left arm and reach my left hand across my body.

I grab Chinzo's left wrist with my left hand.

To break Chinzo's grip on my right wrist, I push down on his left wrist with my left hand and pull my right arm straight back.

Having broken Chinzo's grip on my right wrist, I elevate my right elbow, shift my weight slightly toward my left side, and rotate my shoulders in a counterclockwise direction. Notice how I keep his left arm pinned to his body using my left hand. This not only prevents him from re-forming his grip on my right wrist, but it also keeps him from elevating his arm to block the elbow strike.

Driving my weight forward and continuing to rotate my shoulders, I drop my right elbow into the left side of Chinzo's jaw.

HOOK FROM CLOSED GUARD

This is another simple yet effective technique that you can use when you are kneeling in your opponent's guard and he grabs hold of your wrists. If your goal is to free your right hand, all you have to do is circle your right wrist toward the opening of your opponent's hand while pulling your arm backward. As his grip on your wrist slips away, you are once again free to land strikes with your right arm. However, this technique doesn't involve trapping your opponent's arm to his chest, which means he will still be able to defend your strikes by elevating his arms. While it might still be possible to score with the over-the-top elbow demonstrated in the previous sequence, you'll have a much better chance of landing your strike clean if you employ the looping hook demonstrated below.

I'm in Chinzo's full guard. To prevent me from striking, he has latched on to both of my wrists.

To break Chinzo's left grip on my right wrist, I pull my right arm back while rotating my wrist toward the opening of his left hand. Note, to prevent your opponent from reestablish his grip and blocking your strike, it's important that you throw the punch the instant you free your hand.

I cock my right arm back.

Shifting my weight toward my left side and rotating my shoulders in a counterclockwise direction, I throw a right punch toward Chinzo's face.

Driving my weight forward and continuing to rotate my shoulders, I smash my right fist into the left side of Chinzo's face. It's important to notice how I rotate my fist so that I land with the index and middle knuckles of my right hand.

POSTURE-UP OVERHAND

In this sequence I demonstrate how to set up an earth-shattering punch while kneeling in your opponent's full guard. To begin, post a hand on his chest, elevate one knee off the mat, and then push your body forward. The combination of these three actions not only pins your opponent's shoulders to the mat, but it also allows you to drop your weight down as you throw a punch with your free hand, producing a knockout blow. It is important to note that this elevated position should only be held temporarily. If you remain in it for too long before throwing your punch, your opponent can use the space between your bodies to create a scramble and either work back to his feet or apply a submission.

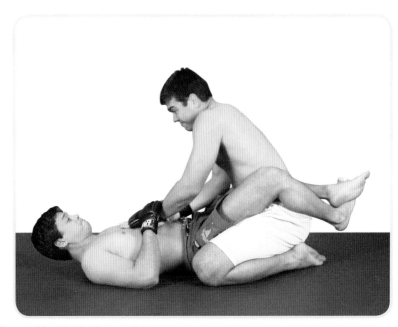

I'm in Chinzo's full guard. To prevent me from striking, he has grabbed both of my wrists.

To break Chinzo's grip on my right wrist, I pull my right arm back while rotating my wrist toward the opening of his left hand. At the same time, I drive my left palm into his chest and post up on my right foot.

Pinning Chinzo's back to the mat using my left hand, I rotate my shoulders in a clockwise direction and cock my right arm back. Notice how I'm leaning slightly forward, placing my weight over my left arm. This prevents him from sitting up to a side and evading my punch.

Pushing off the mat with my right foot, I drive my weight forward, rotate my shoulders in a counterclockwise direction, and throw a right downward punch toward Chinzo's face.

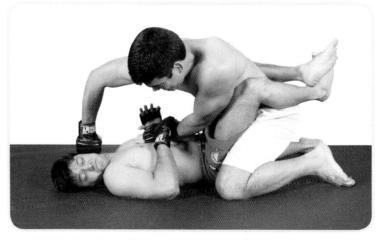

Still driving my weight forward and rotating my shoulders, I smash my right fist into the left side of Chinzo's face. It's important to notice that I lean toward my left side by dropping my left shoulder toward the mat, as well as rotate my fist so that I land with the index and middle knuckles of my right hand. The former adds power to the strike while the latter prevents me from injuring my hand.

KNEE THROUGH THE MIDDLE GUARD PASS

The knee through the middle guard pass is a highly effective technique that can be used anytime you are kneeling in your opponent's open guard. If you look at the photos below, you'll notice that I've elevated my knee to my chest and posted my foot on the mat between my opponent's legs. Whether you force your opponent's guard open with a strike or he opens his guard to attack, you want to immediately assume this position to prevent him from wrapping his legs around your body and trapping you in his closed guard. Once accomplished, your next goal is to secure an underhook on his far side. If you have your right knee elevated, you want to secure a right underhook on his left arm. This not only prevents him from reversing the position or transitioning to your back as you pass through his legs, but it also allows you to flatten his shoulders to the mat as you pass into side control. The nice thing about this technique is it works on all fighters, regardless of their belt rank or grappling experience. Once you secure an underhook and you slide your knee over his thigh, the pass is pretty much in the bag.

I'm in Chinzo's open guard. To prevent him from wrapping his legs around my waist and pulling me into his closed guard, I've sat back onto my left foot and popped my right knee up. From here, I will immediately work to pass his guard into a dominant position.

To prevent me from striking, Chinzo posts his right elbow on the mat and sits up. As he does this, I lean slightly forward, place my left hand on his right knee, and pummel my right arm to the inside of his left arm.

3

Hooking my right arm around the back of Chinzo's left shoulder, I push down on his right knee using my left hand and slide my right knee across the inside of his right thigh.

4

Shifting my weight forward, I slide my right knee through Chinzo's guard and post it on the mat to the outside of his right leg. Notice how this pins his right leg to the mat.

5

With Chinzo's right leg pinned to the mat, I throw my left leg over his right leg and drive my left forearm into the left side of his head.

As I pass my left leg over Chinzo's right leg, I slide my right foot over his right thigh. Notice how my right underhook prevents him from sliding out from underneath my body and circling toward my back.

To secure the side control position, I slide my right leg over Chinzo's right leg, drive my right knee into his right hip, and post my left foot on the mat.

DOWNWARD ELBOW TO OVERHAND

As I mentioned in the introduction to this section, there are countless ground and pound combinations that you can string together from the half guard. In this sequence, I begin my combination by throwing a downward elbow to my opponent's thigh to draw his attention to the lower half of his body, creating an opening for me to immediately follow up with a powerful overhand right to his face. It is important to note that you can also switch up this combination by throwing a punch to your opponent's face to create an opening to land an elbow to his thigh. As long as you keep your opponent's back pinned to the mat, utilize the high/low principle of attack, and capitalize on the openings available, your strikes and targets are a matter of preference.

I'm in Chinzo's half guard, searching for an opening to attack.

Keeping my left arm posted across Chinzo's chest to prevent him from sitting up, I elevate my right arm and prepare to drive a downward elbow into his left thigh.

I drive the tip of my right elbow into Chinzo's left thigh. To inflict the most damage possible, I target his sciatic nerve.

Having shifted Chinzo's focus to the lower half of his body with the downward elbow, I drive my weight forward, rotate my shoulders in a counterclockwise direction, and throw a right overhand toward his face.

Still driving my weight forward and rotating my shoulders, I drop my right fist to the left side of Chinzo's face. It's important to notice that I lean toward my left side by dropping my left shoulder toward the mat, as well as rotate my fist so that I land with the index and middle knuckles of my right hand. The former adds power to the strike while the latter prevents me from injuring my hand.

HEAVY ELBOW FROM HALF GUARD

In this sequence I demonstrate how to land a heavy elbow while in your opponent's half guard. To execute this technique, pin your opponent's back to the mat, posture up, and then drop your weight into your opponent and throw a downward elbow strike to his face. The downside to this technique is that it requires you to momentarily create space between you and your opponent. If he is an exceptional grappler, he can use that space to either sit up into you or roll onto his side. Throwing the strike immediately after posturing cuts down on his defensive options, but when up against a good guard player, a better choice is to keep his shoulders pinned to the mat and utilize short elbow strikes, which I demonstrate in the next sequence.

I'm in Chinzo's half guard, searching for an opening to attack. Notice that I have my hands posted on his chest to keep his back pinned to the mat.

I draw my left arm back and prepare to come down with a powerful left elbow strike.

Rotating my shoulders in a clockwise direction, I drive my weight forward and drive the tip of my left elbow into the left side of Chinzo's face.

SHORT ELBOW FROM HALF GUARD

In this sequence I demonstrate how to pin your opponent's shoulders to the mat from the half guard and land short elbow strikes to his face. Although these blows don't inflict as much damage as the heavy elbow strikes demonstrated in the previous technique, they tend to be a lot safer. If you look at the photos below, you'll notice that I begin by pinning my opponent's left arm to the mat using my right hand to prevent him from sitting up into me and securing an underhook with his left arm. Next, I place my left hand on his chin and press down. As my hand slips off the side of his face, I drive my body weight downward and land a short elbow strike to his jaw.

I'm in Chinzo's half guard. To keep him from sitting up, I pin his left wrist to the mat using my right hand and drive his head into the floor using my left hand.

Driving my weight forward, I rotate my shoulders in a clockwise direction and allow my left hand to slide off Chinzo's face. It's important to note that I keep a portion of my weight distributed over my right arm to keep his left hand pinned to the mat.

Continuing to rotate and drive my weight downward, I strike the right side of Chinzo's face using the tip of my left elbow.

KATA-GATAME (HEAD AND ARM CHOKE)

When you land either a short or heavy elbow from your opponent's half guard, there is a good chance that he will roll away from you to prevent you from landing more strikes. Although this can make it difficult to rain down a series of elbows, it creates a perfect opportunity to transition into the kata-gatame head and arm choke. If you look at the photos below, you'll notice that as my opponent turns away from me, he crosses his near arm over to the far side of his body, making it easy for me to trap his arm against the side of his neck by wrapping my arm around his head. Once accomplished, I pass into side control and tighten down on my lock, forcing his arm into his carotid artery and severing the blood flow to his brain. I know this technique works in competition because I used it to finish judo practitioner Rameau Sokoudjou when we fought in UFC 79.

I'm in Chinzo's half guard, searching for an opening to attack.

I elevate my left arm and prepare to drop an elbow to Chinzo's face.

I land a left elbow to Chinzo's face.

4

To prevent me from landing more strikes, Chinzo raises his right arm and begins turning toward his left side.

5

As Chinzo rolls onto his side, he opens his guard and begins to sit up. To set up the choke and prevent him from escaping, I drop my head and place it against his right shoulder. At the same time, I wrap my right arm underneath his right arm and slide my right hand underneath his head.

6

I drive my weight forward, grip my hands together, and then use my left hand to pull my right arm further underneath Chinzo's head.

7

With Chinzo's right arm trapped to the side of his head, I step my right leg over his right leg and begin to pass his guard into side control.

8

Keeping my weight distributed over Chinzo's right shoulder, I plant my right foot on the mat and transition into side control.

9

I slide my right knee up to Chinzo's right hip and sprawl my left leg straight back.

10

I turn my head and place my chin over Chinzo's right arm. This prevents him from reaching the hand of his trapped arm behind his head and alleviating pressure from the choke. To sever blood flow to his brain, I drop my hips to the mat, squeeze my arms tight, and press my head into his right shoulder.

FIGURE-FOUR ARMLOCK FROM HALF GUARD

In this sequence I demonstrate a highly effective combination from the half guard. With my right leg trapped between my opponent's legs, I turn my back toward his head to gain access to the lower half of his body. Once accomplished, I place my right hand on his left knee and force his leg downward. My goal is to weaken his lock on my trapped leg, allowing me to pass his half guard into a more dominant position such as side control or mount. However, before I can execute the pass, he counters my attack by grabbing my right wrist with his left hand and pulling it away from his knee. Although this makes it difficult for me to force his leg to the mat and escape his half guard, it gives me access to his left arm and allows me to apply the figure-four armlock submission. It is important to note that if your opponent doesn't counter your pass by grabbing your wrist, continue to push down on his leg until you break open his guard. Once accomplished, pass directly into side control or mount.

I'm stuck in Chinzo's half guard. To gain access to the lower half of his body, I've moved my head to the left side of his body and turned my back toward his head.

I cock my right hand back.

In an attempt to weaken Chinzo's lock on my leg, I palm strike his right knee and begin pushing down on his leg. To prevent me from breaking open his guard and passing into a dominant position, Chinzo reaches up and grabs my right wrist with his left hand.

4

Although Chinzo has effectively blocked my pass, I can use his defense to my advantage by transitioning to the figure four-armlock. To set up the submission, I wrap my left arm around the outside of his left arm. Notice how the crook of my arm is positioned just above his left elbow.

5

Rotating my right hand toward the opening of Chinzo's left hand, I pull my right arm back and break his grip on my wrist.

6

Having freed my right arm from Chinzo's grasp, I immediately grab his left wrist with my right hand. Next, I reach my left hand toward my right forearm.

7

I grab my right wrist with my left hand, and then use my figure-four lock to push his left wrist toward the mat. Notice how I rotate my shoulders toward the mat to help me with this process.

8

Continuing to push Chinzo's left hand toward the mat, I slide my weight forward and pull up on his left elbow using my left arm. With a tremendous amount of pressure being placed on his elbow, he has no choice but to tap in submission. It's important to notice how I forcibly turn his wrist so that his thumb is pointing toward the ceiling. This locks his joint in place and allows me to apply the crank to the elbow. If you fail to accomplish this task, the submission will not work.

SLIDE-THROUGH KNEE BAR

In this sequence I demonstrate how to apply the slide-through knee bar when in your opponent's half guard, which comes in handy when you are having trouble landing effective strikes or passing into a more dominant position. Although this is a very effective technique, it is rarely used. The reason for this is because many fighters get too wrapped up in attacking their opponent's upper body. It is important to remember that the high/low principle of attack works just as well on the ground as it does when fighting on your feet. Exclusively attacking your opponent's head and arms with submissions is the same as throwing all your punches and kicks at your opponent's face. By attacking both his legs and upper body, you constantly keep him guessing, which in turn stretches his focus thin and creates openings. However, it is important to note that this technique is not risk free. If you attempt the knee bar and fail to lock in the hold, you can sometimes be left in a compromising position. To limit your risk, I recommend using this technique in the final seconds of a round. That way, if you should miss the submission, your opponent won't have enough time to capitalize on your awkward positioning.

I'm in Chinzo's half guard. Again, I've switched my base so that my back is facing his head, but in this scenario I have positioned my left arm underneath his left arm and hooked my right arm around the inside of his left leg.

I post up on my left hand.

Keeping my body elevated using my left arm, I slide my left knee across Chinzo's belly.

Still using my left arm to keep me elevated, I rotate my body in a clockwise direction, slide my left knee in front of Chinzo's left leg, and hook my left foot around his left hip.

5

I fall to my left hip.

6

Keeping my right arm hooked tight around Chinzo's left leg, I drop to my left side.

7

Pinching my knees together, I clamp my right leg around the inside of Chinzo's left leg and grab his left heel with my left hand.

8

To finish the leglock submission, I slide my right arm up Chinzo's leg, pull his foot toward my chest with both of my hands, curl my right leg tight around his left leg, and thrust my hips into his knee.

STEP-OVER KNEE BAR

Although pinning your opponent's back to the mat when in the top half guard position is ideal, it isn't always possible due to the defensive options at his disposal. In the sequence below, my opponent employs one of the most common defensives by turning onto his side. This makes it difficult to utilize many of the striking techniques already demonstrated, but it creates an opportunity to transition into the step-over knee bar. The key to success with this technique is keeping his near arm glued to his side and his far shoulder pinned to the mat. If you allow him to sit up into you and secure an underhook, his escape and attack options increase dramatically, making the submission hard to apply. Just as with the other leglocks shown, there is always the risk of losing your dominant positioning should you fail with the submission. As a result, it is best utilized in the last seconds of a round.

Chinzo has my right leg trapped in his half guard and he has turned into me by rolling onto his right side. Notice how I keep his left arm pinned to his body using my right arm. If you allow your opponent to sit up into you and secure an underhook, the knee bar will be difficult to execute. In addition to this, your opponent will also have dramatically increased his offensive options.

In one fluid motion, I post both of my hands on the mat to the right side of Chinzo's body, turn my shoulders and hips in a counterclockwise direction, and step my left leg over the top of his legs.

Continuing to rotate my body in a counterclockwise direction, I balance on my right hand, step my left leg over Chinzo's left leg, and plant my left foot on the mat on his left side.

4

I lean slightly forward, wrap my left arm around the outside of Chinzo's left calf, and sit my butt toward the mat.

5

Pulling Chinzo's left leg toward my chest, I fall to my left hip and slide my left leg underneath his left leg.

6

Still pulling Chinzo's left leg toward my chest, I fall toward my left side.

7

As I fall onto my left side, I slide my left hand up Chinzo's left leg and cup his ankle. At the same time, I hook my left leg over my right foot and squeeze my knees together, tapping his leg.

8

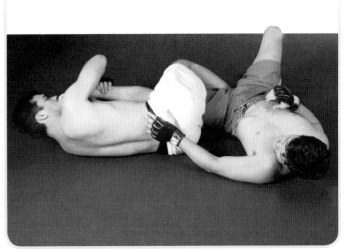

To finish the knee bar, I grab Chinzo's left heel with my right hand and then use both of my hands to pull his leg toward my chest. At the same time, I pinch my knees together and thrust my hips into his knee. The combination of these actions puts a tremendous amount of pressure on his knee, forcing him to tap out in submission.

COUNTER KIMURA TO FAR-SIDE ARMBAR

When you pass into the half guard, a lot of opponent's will roll onto their side and lock in a kimura on your near arm before you can pin their back to the mat and start your assault. In this sequence, I demonstrate how to counter this common scenario by stepping your free leg over your trapped arm, which eliminates the leverage he needs to crank your arm behind your back. Next, I demonstrate how to use his lock on your arm to your advantage by transitioning into a straight armbar. This is accomplished by stepping over his head, pinning his arm to your chest, and then hyperextending his arm by driving your hips upward into his elbow. The key to success with this technique is employing the counter the instant your opponent locks in the kimura. If you delay, he can use his lock to submit you from his half guard or reverse your positioning by forcing you into a forward roll.

Technical Note: Sometimes when you circle around your opponent's head to secure the armlock, he will keep your leg trapped in his guard. Although freeing your leg before executing the armbar is ideal, it isn't necessary for pulling off the submission. As long as you step your free leg to the opposite side of your opponent's head and get your hips underneath his elbow, you should have no problem locking in the armbar.

As I passed into Chinzo's half guard, he grabbed my right wrist with his left hand.

Before I can pin Chinzo's back to the mat and lock down the position, he sits up, posts his left elbow on the mat, and wraps his right arm around the back of my right arm.

As Chinzo wraps his right arm around the back of my right arm to lock in the kimura, I immediately slide my right leg forward and reach my right hand underneath my thigh.

Continuing to slide my right leg up, I hook my right hand underneath my right thigh.

Having hooked my right hand underneath my right thigh, I drop my right knee to the mat, drive my weight forward, and pin Chinzo's back to the mat. This strips him of his leverage and prevents him from applying the crank on my arm.

6

Now that I have effectively defended the kimura, I can use Chinzo's lock to my advantage and transition to a far-side armbar. To begin this process, I post up on my left foot, turn my body in a counterclockwise direction, and slide my right leg over the top of his head.

7

Still corkscrewing my body in a counterclockwise direction, I slide my right knee underneath Chinzo's right arm.

8

Continuing to corkscrew my body in a counterclockwise direction, I sit my butt to the mat and pull my left leg out from in between Chinzo's legs.

9

I clamp my left leg over the top of Chinzo's head and pull his right arm toward my chest using my right hand.

10

Leaning back slightly, I grab Chinzo's right arm with my left hand, pull my right knee out from underneath his right arm, and hook my right foot underneath his right shoulder.

11

Adjusting Chinzo's right hand so that his thumb is pointing toward the ceiling, I pull his arm toward my chest using both of my hands, pinch my knees together, and thrust my hips upward into his elbow.

PART FIVE
ATTACKS FROM DOMINANT CONTROL

In this section, I demonstrate several highly effective attacks from the most dominant positions on the ground—side control, the mount, and back control. From each position, I show you how to stabilize the control to prevent your opponent from escaping, throw strikes without compromising your position, and set up fight-ending submissions. Although these sections are far from complete, each technique I offer has been proved to work at the highest level of competition. Instead of putting in a bunch of filler, I included only the techniques that I use on a regular basis in my fights and training.

5-1: Side Control Attacks

Side control is a very powerful position in MMA. Although it is possible to pin your opponent's back to the mat while in his full and half guard, doing so from the top side control position not only provides you with numerous options to attack, but it also leaves your opponent with very few. And unlike the mount and back positions, side control is a very difficult position for your opponent to escape from. With your weight positioned over his torso, it becomes hard for him to execute a rolling or shrimping maneuver to pull you into his guard. For this reason, I suggest spending an ample amount of time practicing the techniques in this section. Once you have them mastered, the next step is to learn how to use your striking options to set up your submission options.

5-2: Mount Attacks

The mount is the most dominant position in MMA because it allows you to effectively pin your opponent's back to the mat while remaining in the postured-up position. This gives you the freedom to rain down powerful strikes without losing your ability to transition into a fight-ending submission. However, the mount is easier for your opponent to reverse than when you are in the top side control position, making it important to pay close attention to your base at all times. If your opponent manages to shrimp his hips free, instead of continuing with your strikes, take a moment to reestablish your base. This can be accomplished by hooking your feet underneath his legs and thrusting your hips forward. Once you've stabilized the position, you can immediately return to throwing strikes or begin setting up a submission.

5-3: Back Attacks

Although back control doesn't offer the same amount of striking opportunities as either mount or side control, it provides you with several high-percentage submissions. In this section, I cover some of my favorite techniques to execute. As you will see on the coming pages, all the techniques are performed with my opponent's body on top of mine. It is from this position that you have the best chance of locking in a submission. Personally, I like to always attempt to apply the rear naked choke first. It is a dangerous submission that can bring the fight to a dramatic close. However, a lot of opponents are masters at defending against the rear naked choke, so I also provide several submissions that you can transition into when up against such an opponent, including an armbar and a kata-gatame choke.

GROUND AND POUND TACTICS FROM SIDE CONTROL

Striking from the top side control position is not only an excellent way to create openings for submissions, but it can also create opportunities to transition into other dominant controls such as mount and back. While it is possible to get quite creative with your strikes from side control, you must keep your opponent's shoulders pinned to the mat. If you posture up to land devastating blows, your opponent can use the newly created space to scramble up to his feet, pull you into his guard, or reverse your positioning with a sweep. To prevent such an outcome, you have two primary options—utilize one of the techniques demonstrated later in this section to transition to either the mount or the knee-on-belly position, both of which allow you to posture up with much less risk, or create opportunities to land strikes directly from side control using one of the two modified positions demonstrated in the sequence below. Although both of these controls allow you to keep your opponent's shoulders pinned to the mat, you will dramatically increase your ground and pound success by learning how to transition back and forth between them. When your opponent begins to defend your strikes from one position, you transition to the other, and vice versa. It is important to remember that position is the most important thing. Never throw strikes unless you have the position locked down. If you get overeager and allow space to come between your bodies, your opponent will most likely employ an escape, stripping you of your dominant position.

I've secured side control on Chinzo's right side. It's important to notice my base. I'm facing his head, my right hip is flush to the mat, my right knee is positioned underneath his right shoulder, and I've secured a right underhook. With the majority of my weight distributed over his torso, he is unable to sit up or roll onto a side to escape. From here, I will immediately start delivering strikes with my left arm to create openings to attack.

Keeping my weight distributed over Chinzo's torso, I cock my left arm back.

3

Twisting my shoulders slightly, I drop my left fist into the right side of Chinzo's face.

4

 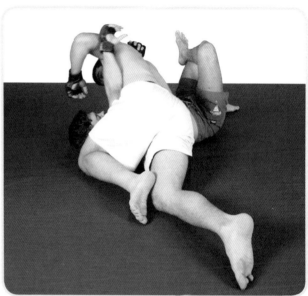

To capitalize on Chinzo's stunned state, I rotate my hips in a counterclockwise direction, bring my right leg underneath my left leg, and throw my left leg over my right leg. As I switch my base, I slide my left knee up to the right side of his head and trap his arm between my leg and hip. This prevents him from wedging his elbow to the inside of my hips, creating space, and escaping the position. To keep his back pinned to the mat as I make my transition, I keep a large percentage of my weight on his torso.

5

I maneuver my left arm to the left side of Chinzo head and slide my right knee up to his right hip.

6

Having switched my base, I elevate my left arm and prepare to drop an elbow down into the left side of Chinzo's face. It's important to notice how I keep my head low and use my right underhook to keep my opponent's left arm to the side of my head. This not only prevents him from blocking the strikes to follow, but it also keeps him from pummeling his left arm to the inside of my right arm, getting up to his side, and then creating a scramble.

7

Keeping Chinzo's right arm trapped to the right side of his head, I bring my left arm down and drive the tip of my elbow into his left temple.

KNEE-ON-BELLY

As I mentioned in the previous sequence, the knee-on-belly is an excellent position from which to rain down powerful strikes such as elbows, downward punches, and hammer fists. The only downside to establishing knee-on-belly is that it creates space between you and your opponent, making it easier for him to escape. To avoid losing your dominant top position, I recommend that you use it sparingly. For example, slide your knee over your opponent's body to secure knee-on-belly, land a couple of hard shots, and then pass your knee to the opposite side of his body and secure the mount position. Another example would be to pop up into the knee-on-belly position from side control, land a couple of hard strikes, and then quickly regain control of his body by transitioning back into side control. As I have mentioned, if you jeopardize your positioning for the sake of landing a few extra hard shots, you give your opponent a chance to escape your control. By using knee-on-belly as a transitional position, you will have a lot of success at throwing off your opponent's defenses and creating openings to attack.

I've secured the knee-on-belly position by sliding my right knee across Chinzo's abdomen and posting up on my left leg. To keep my opponent from sitting up and turning into me to escape, I've secured a right underhook and I'm driving my left hand down into his face.

I elevate my left hand and prepare to drop a heavy left elbow down into Chinzo's face.

Using the weight of my body to add power to the strike, I drop the tip of my left elbow into Chinzo's face. It's important to mention that in addition to being able to throw a heavy elbow as shown here, you also have the option of throwing a downward punch or hammer fist. Personally, I like to throw the elbow because it is safe and inflicts the most damage.

KIMURA

In this sequence I demonstrate how to apply the kimura submission from side control. To set up the technique, the first step is to immobilize your opponent's defenses. If you've secured side control on his right side, this can be accomplished by stepping your left leg over his head, putting you in the north-south position. With his shoulders pinned heavily to the mat, he will be unable to defend against the submission by sitting up or rolling onto his knees. The next step is to secure a figure-four lock on his far arm and then crank his wrist toward his far shoulder. When applied correctly, it puts a tremendous amount of pressure on his shoulder and elbow, forcing him to tap in submission. To increase your success at locking in the submission, I strongly suggest setting it up using the ground and pound techniques demonstrated earlier in this section. The great part about this technique is that once you have stepped over your opponent's head and properly secured control of his arm, he has little chance of escaping, making it a high percentage submission.

I've secured side control on Chinzo's right side. It's important to notice my base. I'm facing his head, my right hip is flush to the mat, my right knee is positioned underneath his right shoulder, and I've secured a right underhook. With the majority of my weight distributed over his torso, he is unable to sit up or roll onto a side to escape.

Rotating my body in a clockwise direction, I place my left hand on the mat and throw my left leg over my right leg.

3

Keeping my weight distributed over Chinzo's upper body, I plant my left knee on the mat to the left side of his head. It's important to notice that by rolling onto my knees, I've trapped his right arm across his neck. This prevents him from wrapping his right arm around my back and scrambling out of the position.

4

Having trapped Chinzo's right arm and head between my legs, I pull his left arm to my chest using my right underhook and then wrap my left arm around the inside of his left arm.

5

As I release my right underhook, I slide my left arm up Chinzo's left arm so that the crook of my left arm is flush with the crook of his left arm.

To secure the figure-four lock on Chinzo's arm, I grab his left wrist with my right hand and then grab the top of my right wrist with my left hand.

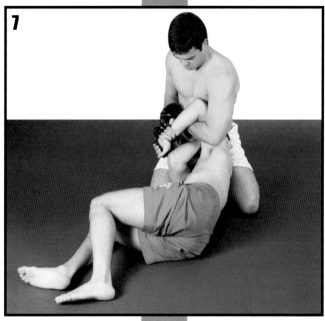

Keeping Chinzo's left arm flush with my chest, I posture up and pull his left arm upward.

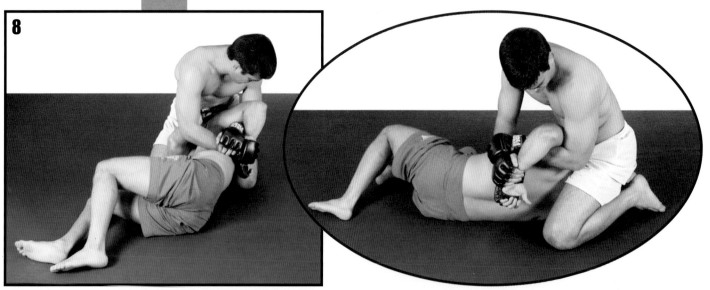

To apply the kimura submission, I twist my upper body in a counterclockwise direction, pull up on his left arm using my left arm, and drive his left hand toward my left knee using my right hand. My actions put a tremendous amount of pressure on his left shoulder and elbow, forcing him to tap.

SIDE CONTROL TO MOUNT TRANSITION

There are several ways for transitioning from side control into the mount. A lot of fighters will attempt to make the transition by simply stepping their leg over their opponent's body. While this method will sometimes work, there is a large chance that your opponent will trap one of your legs, putting you in his half guard. In my opinion, a much better approach is to utilize the knee-over-belly pass demonstrated in the sequence below. The key to being successful with this technique is remaining tight to your opponent throughout the transition. If there is space between your bodies, your opponent gains the ability to scramble and possibly escape.

1

I've secured the side control position with over-under control on Chinzo's right side. Notice how he has his right knee elevated to hinder me from stepping my leg over his body and securing the mount.

2

Distributing my weight over my left shoulder, I elevate my hips and slide my right knee to the inside of Chinzo's right leg.

3

I slide my right knee across Chinzo's belly.

4

Pressing my weight forward to keep Chinzo's shoulders pinned, I slide my right knee down to the mat. It is important to notice that I have his left arm trapped. If you allow your opponent to free his arm, he will most likely drive his left hand into your right knee, climb up to his side, and escape to his half guard.

5

To secure the mount, I drop my right leg to the mat and pinch my knees together. From here, I will immediately posture up and get my offense going with some ground and pound.

GROUND AND POUND TACTICS FROM MOUNT

When you properly secure the mount position, your opponent's back gets pinned to the mat, allowing you to posture up and use the weight of your body to deliver ruthless punches and elbow strikes. Where a lot of fighters go wrong with the mount is they attempt to strike before controlling their opponent. To limit my opponent's defenses, I like to wrap one hand around his throat and pin his head to the mat. This prevents him from sitting up into me, wrapping his arms around my body, and then putting me on my back by bridging me over his shoulder. If he should wiggle free from this control, I will take a break from throwing strikes with my free arm and work on reestablishing the position. With the mount often taking a lot of hard work to reach, the last thing you want to do is lose the position due to over eagerness.

1) I've secured the mount position on Chinzo. To position myself to throw strikes, I wrap my left hand around his throat, posture up, and distribute my weight forward to keep his shoulders pinned to the mat and his head stationary. 2) Keeping a portion of my weight distributed over my left arm, I cock my right arm back and prepare to unleash a ground and pound assault. 3) Rotating my shoulders in a counterclockwise direction, I shift my weight forward and drive my right fist into Chinzo's face. 4) Continuing my ground and pound assault, I posture up and cock my right arm back. 5) Without hesitating, I rotate my shoulders in a counterclockwise direction and shift my weight forward just as I did with the punch, only this time I come down with a heavy elbow to Chinzo's chin.

ARMBAR FROM MOUNT

After you've landed several hard punches or elbows from the mount position, your opponent will most likely elevate his arms in an attempt to protect his face from your barrage of strikes. When this occurs, you can either continue to throw downward strikes or execute the armbar demonstrated in the sequence below. If you choose the armbar, it is very important to transition into the submission in one fluid motion. If you stall or give up space between your bodies, your opponent will have a much greater chance of defending against the submission.

1

I've secured the mount position. Notice how Chinzo has elevated his arms to protect his face from strikes. Instead of throwing more punches and elbows, I will use his defense to my advantage by transitioning to an armbar.

2

To position myself for the armbar, I place my hands on the mat above Chinzo's head and pull my knees and hips up his body.

3

I slide my knees up until they pass Chinzo's shoulders. Once in position, I pinch my knees together and start to posture up.

4

With Chinzo's arms trapped to his head, I shift a larger portion of my weight onto my right knee, rotate my body in a counterclockwise direction, and straighten my left leg out to my side.

5

Still rotating my body in a counterclockwise direction, I hook my left leg around Chinzo's right shoulder and wedge my right hand underneath his left forearm.

6

I wrap my right arm around Chinzo's left arm and pull it toward my chest.

Curling my left leg into Chinzo's right shoulder, I lean my upper body forward and throw my right leg over the top of his head.

I slide my right foot over Chinzo's head and to the right side of his body. It's important to mention that you always want to throw your leg over your opponent's head before laying your back to the mat to apply the armbar. If you fail to do this, your opponent will sit up into you as you drop to the mat, not only escaping the armbar, but also reversing the position.

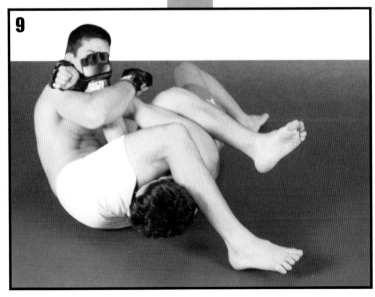

As I hook my right leg around Chinzo's head, I roll to my back and slide my right arm up his left arm.

To finish the armbar, I curl my legs into Chinzo's right side, pull his left hand into my chest using my right arm, and thrust my hips into his elbow. With his arm hyperextending, he has no choice but to tap.

FINISHING OPTION 2

If you have trouble hyperextending your opponent's arm using the technique demonstrated in the previous sequence, grab his wrist using both hands and then use your control to pull his arm into your chest. This form of control not only provides you with more leverage, but it also allows you to position your opponent's thumb toward the ceiling, which is mandatory for finishing the submission.

Unable to finish the armbar using the previous technique, I latch on to Chinzo's wrist with both of my hands and then pull his arm into my chest. With his thumb pointed toward the ceiling and his elbow hyperextended, I finish the submission by curling my legs into his right side and thrusting my hips into his elbow.

REAR NAKED CHOKE

In this sequence I demonstrate how to secure the rear naked choke from the back position. To increase your success with this powerful submission, there are a few guidelines you must follow. First, spread your opponent's legs apart by hooking your feet to the inside of his legs. A lot of fighters have the bad habit of crossing their feet. This is not recommended because not only does it allow your opponent to position his feet close together, which gives him mobility and leverage, but it also allows him to apply a quick leglock by hooking his leg over your feet. Second, establish the over-under control by securing an underhook with one arm, hooking your opposite arm over his shoulder, and then clasping your hands together in the center of his chest. Establishing this grip allows you to control your opponent's upper body, which prevents him from rolling into you and escaping the position. Third, when setting up the choke, don't let your opponent gain control of your arms. If he defends by pulling your choking arm down and away from his neck, immediately attack his neck using your opposite arm. If he drives his chin to his chest to prevent you from sliding your forearm across his throat, grab his nose and pull his head up. Remember, the majority of the time it's a dogfight to secure the rear naked choke, so it is imperative that you stay on the offensive until an opening presents itself. Finally, always position the hand of your lever arm behind your opponent's head. Placing your hand on the top of his head will sometimes work, but it is very easy for your opponent to defend against. If you can't place the back of your hand behind his head because you are wearing MMA gloves, cupping the palm of your lever arm behind his head will usually do the trick. As long as you follow these guidelines, and then squeeze your arms tight once the submission is applied, you will have good success at finishing your opponent with this devastating choke.

I've secured control of Chinzo's back. My feet are hooked to the inside of his thighs and I'm applying outward pressure to his legs. To set up the rear naked choke, I've hooked my left hand over his left wrist and pulled his arm down. I've also managed to wedge my right forearm underneath his neck.

Having set up the rear choke, I release my control on Chinzo's left arm and quickly bring my left hand up toward his head.

3

Before Chinzo can bring his left arm up to defend against the choke, I cross my left hand over the top of my right hand and wedge it behind his head.

4

I latch on to my left biceps with my right hand and hook my left hand behind Chinzo's head. As I mention in the introduction, ideally you want the knuckles of your left hand to be flush with your opponent's head. However, achieving this task is difficult to manage due to the padding on the MMA gloves. As long as you have your hand positioned behind your opponent's head, he will have a hard time defending against the choke.

5

To finish the choke, I tuck my chin toward my chest and drive my head into my left hand. At the same time, I squeeze my arms together with all my might, forcing Chinzo to tap out.

ARMBAR

When I secure the back position, I will always open my attack with a rear naked choke. Although securing this submission is ideal, a lot of fighters are absolute masters at defending against it. If I encounter such an opponent, I will move on to another submission, such as the armbar demonstrated in the sequence below. It is important to note that in order to apply the technique properly, your opponent must be positioned on top of you, as mine is in the first photo. If he rolls to his side, your leg will be trapped, making it next to impossible to transition into the armbar.

I've secured control of Chinzo's back.

Chinzo is doing a good job defending against the choke. Rather than waste energy fighting for the submission, I immediately start setting up an armbar. To begin, I maneuver my right arm to the left side of his head and then wedge my hand in the crevice of his neck so that the back of my forearm is flush with his head.

Maintaining outward pressure on Chinzo's legs using both of my legs, I drive my forearm into his head, forcing him toward my right side. At the same time, I hook my left arm around the inside of his left arm.

I grab Chinzo's left wrist with my right hand. Next, I grab my right forearm with my left hand.

5

Having isolated Chinzo's left arm, I swing my right leg toward his head.

6

As I swing my right leg over Chinzo's head, I turn my body in a clockwise direction.

7

Having maneuvered my body out from underneath Chinzo's body, I hook my right leg around the left side of his head and apply downward pressure. At the same time, I reposition my left leg across his abdomen.

8

Still applying downward pressure to Chinzo's head using my right leg, I sit up and force his back to the mat.

9

Curling my legs inward to keep Chinzo from rolling onto his side, I pull his arm to my chest using my arms and fall to my back.

10

To finish the armbar, I grab his wrist with both of my hands, pull his hand into my chest, and thrust my hips into his elbow. When applying this submission, it's important that you position your opponent's thumb toward the ceiling as shown here.

KATA-GATAME (HEAD AND ARM CHOKE)

When you secure back control and your opponent either defends against the rear naked choke or attempts to roll into you to escape to your guard, the kata-gatame choke is an excellent submission to transition into. In either scenario, the first step is to release one of your hooks. For example, if you are setting up the choke on his right side or he rolls toward his right to escape, remove your left foot off his left hip and hook it underneath his left leg. This allows you to extend your foot into his leg, which not only prevents him from driving his foot off the mat and turning into you, but it also allows you to slide your body out from underneath his body, trap his arm to the side of his neck, and sever blood flow to his brain by applying the choke.

1

I've secured control of Chinzo's back.

2

Chinzo is doing a good job defending against the rear naked choke. Instead of wasting energy fighting for the submission, I will transition to the kata-gatame choke. To begin, I circle my left leg around his left leg and hook my left foot underneath his left knee. Notice that I have my right arm hooked underneath his right arm.

3

To strip Chinzo of his leverage, I extend my left leg into his left leg. At the same time, I release my left grip on his left arm and begin sliding my body out from underneath his body.

4

As I slide out from underneath Chinzo's body, I turn into him and wrap my right arm underneath his right arm and around the left side of his neck. Once accomplished, I grip my hands together over his right shoulder to trap his right arm to the right side of his head. As I do this, I pull my left leg out from underneath his body and throw my right leg over the top of his right leg.

5

Still turning into my opponent, I pull my left leg out from underneath Chinzo's left leg and then slide it under my right leg. Next, I secure the side control position by driving my right knee up to his right hip.

6

To finish the choke, I drop my hips to the mat, squeeze my arms tight, and press my head into Chinzo's right shoulder. An important detail worth noting is how I turn my head and place my chin over his right arm. This locks his arm in place and prevents him from defending the choke by reaching the hand of his trapped arm behind his head.

PART SIX
THE GUARD

This section is devoted to the bottom guard positions. Whether you are playing closed guard, open guard, half guard, or butterfly guard, there are two rules you must follow to be effective. The first rule is to control distance. Ideally, you want to close off all space between you and your opponent to stifle his attacks. For example, if your opponent is in your closed guard, this can be accomplished by grabbing his head and pulling his body down on top of you. If he is in your half guard, it can be accomplished by rolling into him, sitting up to your side, and establishing an underhook. If he is in your butterfly guard, you can close off all space by sitting up into him, securing an underhook and an overhook, and

then positioning your head underneath his chin on the opposite side of your underhook. With each of these techniques, you close off all space between your bodies, which not only makes it very difficult for your opponent to throw strikes, but it also allows you to attack his body with sweeps and submissions.

Although closing off space is ideal, it isn't always possible. Sometimes your opponent will posture up or push you away to create the space he needs to throw strikes. If he doesn't allow you to rebreak his posture, it can be in your best interest to create even more separation so that he cannot reach you with his strikes. If your opponent is in your closed guard when he postures up, you can create separation by opening your

Closing off space in the butterfly guard.

Creating space from half guard.

guard, placing your feet on his hips, and positioning your knees in front of his shoulders. If he is in your half guard, you can create space by sliding your free leg to the inside of his body and driving your knee into his chest.

When you put up these distance-creating barriers, your opponent will often attempt to get past them by driving back into you, but this can be a positive reaction because it once again allows you to obtain control of his body and close off all space. As long as you can transition back and forth between closing off space and creating space, you can keep your opponent at bay while you set up your attacks.

The second rule to being effective from the bottom guard positions is to remain active. When you are fighting from your back you always want to work for three things: a submission, a sweep, or getting back up to your feet. If your opponent defends a sweep, use his defense to transition to a submission. If he defends the submission, use his defensive positioning to climb back up to your feet. The combinations that you can string together are endless. The important thing is to always move and always attack. When you are on the offensive, your opponent's attention is focused on defense, which not only makes it difficult for him to keep up with your movement, but it also makes it difficult for him to launch an attack of his own.

In this section, you will learn my favorite techniques from the full guard, open guard, half guard, and butterfly guard. In addition to showing several submissions, I've also included a number of sweeps and methods for climbing back up to the standing position. Although there are countless attacks that you can execute from the guard, I've chosen to include the techniques that have worked best for me over the years.

STRIKING FROM OPEN GUARD

In this sequence I demonstrate a couple of strikes that you can employ when you have an opponent in your open guard. Although these strikes don't cause much damage, they are excellent for distracting your opponent from landing strikes of his own or passing your guard. In addition to this, they are also an excellent tool to help you set up the attacks demonstrated later in this section. Remember, the key is to stay busy to prevent your opponent from implementing his game plan. By throwing strikes to his face, you shift his focus from an offensive mind-set to a defensive one, creating openings to attack in the process.

1

I've established the open guard position on Chinzo. To maintain distance and prevent him from striking, I place both of my feet on his hips and wrap my left arm over the top of his arms. From here, I will distract him with strikes so that I can set up a sweep, submission, or work my way back up to my feet.

2

As I extend my legs into Chinzo's hips, I twist my shoulders in a counterclockwise direction and throw a right punch toward his face.

3

I land my right punch to the left side of Chinzo's jaw.

4

I roll onto my left shoulder and cock my right arm behind my head.

5

With a clenched fist, I chop my right hand into the right side of Chinzo's jaw. Having landed a couple of strikes to his face, I will now use his disoriented state to my advantage by getting back up to my feet, setting up a submission, or executing a sweep

GET UP FROM GUARD

When you have an aggressive opponent in your full guard, he will often attempt to stand up to either throw powerful punches to your body and head or create openings to pass into a more dominant position. In the sequence below, I demonstrate how to prevent him from achieving his goal by placing your feet on his hips as he labors to his feet and then pushing him away to create distance, giving you an opportunity to escape to your feet. The key to success with this technique is exploding up to your feet the instant you drive your opponent away and create distance. If you hesitate, he will close the distance you created and immediately launch a counterattack. It is also important to note that this technique isn't restricted to this particular scenario. It can be utilized effectively anytime you manage to position your feet on your opponent's hips when he is in your open guard.

I've got Chinzo in my closed guard.

To improve his position and get his offense going, Chinzo leans his upper body forward, places his hands on my chest, and then begins climbing to his feet. Utilizing the space he created, I unlock my guard and place both of my feet on his hips.

As Chinzo stands up, I drive my feet into his hips and extend my legs.

Having created distance with my previous actions, I sit up, post my left hand on the mat, and slide my left foot underneath my right leg. Notice that I keep my right arm extended. This not only allows me to gauge distance, but it also helps protect my face against potential strikes.

I coil my right leg inward and place my right foot directly in front of my left foot.

Driving off the mat with my left hand and right foot, I elevate my hips and pull my left leg out from underneath my body.

Keeping my right hand up to protect my face, I plant my left foot on the mat and secure a solid base.

I assume my fighting stance and immediately start searching for an opening to attack.

ARMBAR

When you have an opponent in your full guard, he will sometimes wrap his hands around the back of your head and apply a neck crank by forcing your chin toward your chest. Even though this submission isn't that effective, it can still be painful and restrict your movement. To counter this hold, immediately hook an arm over his arms and transition to the armbar demonstrated in the sequence below. While neck cranks of this nature are rare in jiu-jitsu competition, they are quite common in MMA, making it a good counter to have in your arsenal. It is important to note that this technique isn't just a counter. Anytime your opponent's elbows are positioned to the inside of your hips, such as when he places his hands on your chest, you have the option to transition into the submission.

Chinzo is in my closed guard. In an effort to restrict my movement, he has wrapped both of his hands around the back of my head.

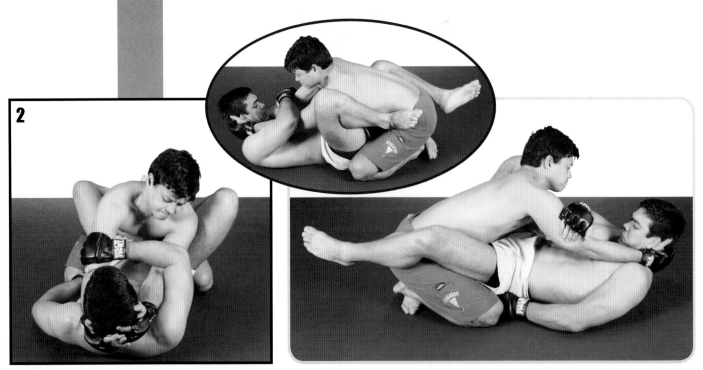

To capitalize on Chinzo's mistake, I will immediately transition to the armbar. To begin this process, I wrap my right arm over the top of his arms and grab the back of his right triceps, trapping his left arm. At the same time, I unlock my guard, place my right foot on his left hip, and wedge my left hand to the inside of his right knee.

I rotate my body in a clockwise direction by pushing off Chinzo's left hip using my right foot and pulling on his left arm using my right hand. Notice how this moves my hips underneath his left elbow.

As I rotate my body, I begin to swing my right leg over Chinzo's head.

Still rotating my body in a clockwise direction, I swing my right leg to the right side of Chinzo's face.

6

I wrap my right leg around the right side of Chinzo's head. When executing this armbar, it's important that you apply independent pressure on your opponent's body and head with both of your legs. A lot of fighters make the mistake of crossing their feet when they achieve this position. Doing so not only gives up space, but it also restricts the control you have over your opponent's posture, which dramatically decreases your chances of completing the submission.

7

Applying downward pressure on Chinzo's body and head with both of my legs to control his posture, I maneuver my left hand out from underneath his right leg.

8

Having freed my left arm, I grab Chinzo's left wrist with my left hand, cup my right hand over my left hand, and then position his arm so that his thumb is facing the ceiling. To finish the armbar, I apply downward pressure on his body and head with my legs, pull his arm into my chest, and thrust my hips into his elbow. These actions cause his arm to hyperextend, forcing him to tap in submission.

ARMBAR TO OMAPLATA SWEEP

In this sequence I demonstrate how to transition to the omaplata sweep and put your opponent on his back when he defends against the armbar demonstrated in the previous sequence. Remember, you always want to remain on the offensive by stringing your attacks together into combinations. For every technique your opponent defends against, another opening to attack is created. It is important to note that while it is possible to transition from the armlock into the omaplata submission, due the sweat and lack of control when grappling without a gi, it can be a little risky to attempt. Rather than going for the submission and possibly losing your control, a better option is to sweep your opponent to his back and then work to finish him from side control, which offers a number of high percentage submissions.

Chinzo is in my closed guard. In an effort to restrict my movement, he has wrapped both of his hands around the back of my head.

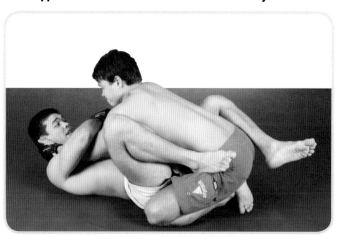

To capitalize on Chinzo's mistake, I will immediately transition to the armbar. To begin this process, I wrap my right arm over the top of his arms and grab the back of his right triceps, trapping his left arm. At the same time, I unlock my guard, place my right foot on his left hip, and wedge my left hand to the inside of his right knee.

Using my right foot to push off Chinzo's left hip and my right hand to pull on his left arm, I rotate my body in a clockwise direction and maneuver my hips underneath his left elbow.

4

Keen to my intentions, Chinzo pulls his left arm out from between my legs before I can apply the submission. Instead of giving up on my attack, I will immediately transition to the omaplata.

5

Still using my left arm to rotate my body in a clockwise direction, I hook my left leg around the back of Chinzo's right shoulder.

6

I hook my right leg over my left foot and then grab Chinzo's right wrist with my right hand. Notice how I have my left arm wrapped around the inside of his right leg. This control will allow me to force him into a forward roll as I sit up.

To force Chinzo into a forward roll, I sit up to my right hip, post my right elbow on the mat and rotate my shoulders in a clockwise direction. To prevent a scramble from ensuing as he rolls to his back, I maintain control of his right leg with my left arm.

Continuing with my previous actions, I pop up to my right knee.

As Chinzo rolls to his back, I plant my left knee on the mat and begin posturing up. From here, I will immediately work to secure the side control position.

KIMURA

Anytime your opponent places his hands on the mat while in your full guard, he becomes vulnerable to sweeps and sub-missions. In the sequence below I demonstrate how to capitalize on this mistake by applying a kimura, one of the most effective submissions that you can execute from this position. When studying the photos, pay special attention to how I set up the lock and apply the finishing hold. If you fly through the technique without focusing on every detail, your chances of securing a proper hold on your opponent's arm and pulling off the submission are very low.

Chinzo is in my closed guard with his hands on the mat. To capitalize on his positioning, I grab his right wrist with my left hand and wrap my right hand around the back of his neck.

In order to secure the kimura on Chinzo's right arm, I have to move his head toward my right side and sit up toward my left. To accomplish these tasks, I pull down on his head with my right hand and then begin pushing it to my right side. As I clear his head from my body, I unlock my guard and start sitting up. It's important to note that if you don't clear your opponent's head from your body, he will most likely nullify your attack by planting his forehead on your chest and pinning your shoulders to the mat.

In one fluid motion, I sit up to my left elbow, wrap my right arm around the back of Chinzo's right arm, and then start pushing his right wrist backward with my left hand.

I grab my left wrist with my right hand, fall to my left shoulder, and begin cranking Chinzo's right arm behind his body. It's important to notice that I've escaped my upper body out from under his upper body by shrimping my hips in a clockwise direction.

Driving my right leg into Chinzo's left leg to help with the clockwise rotation of my hips, I roll onto my right shoulder and throw my left leg over his back to keep his posture broken. To finish the kimura, I pull my right arm into my body while driving my left hand in the direction of his head. This puts a tremendous amount of pressure on his elbow and shoulder, forcing him to tap in submission.

KIMURA SWEEP

When you apply the kimura on an opponent in your full guard, he will sometimes counter by wrapping his arms around your waist and driving his weight forward. Although this can make it difficult to finish the submission, it creates an opportunity to transition to the kimura sweep and put your opponent on his back. However, due to the predictable nature of this counter, it is important that you treat the kimura and kimura sweep as one move. If your opponent defends against the kimura submission, you transition seamlessly to the kimura sweep. If he should defend against the kimura sweep, you transition seamlessly back to the kimura submission. As long as you remain on the offensive, you will eventually get one step ahead of your opponent and be successful with your attack.

Chinzo is in my closed guard with his hands on the mat. To capitalize on his positioning, I grab his right wrist with my left hand and wrap my right hand around the back of his neck.

In one fluid motion, I unlock my guard, sit up to my left elbow, and wrap my right arm around the back of Chinzo's right arm. To defend against the kimura submission, Chinzo wraps his right arm around my body and drives his weight forward.

3 Instead of fighting for the kimura submission, I immediately transition to the kimura sweep by hooking my right hand over the top of Chinzo's right wrist. This not only gives me the leverage to carry him over with the sweep, but it will also prevent him from posting his right hand to the mat and blocking the sweep.

4 I coil my right leg inward and plant my right foot on the mat. At the same time, I bring my left knee toward my chest and slide it down to Chinzo's right knee.

5 To land a successful sweep, I first have to shatter Chinzo's base. I accomplish this by driving my left leg downward into his right knee.

6

As I drive my left leg down into Chinzo's right knee, I rotate my hips in a counterclockwise direction and elevate my right leg into his left side. The combination of these actions strips him of his base and forces him to roll toward his back.

7

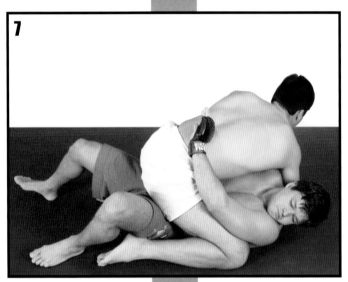

I follow Chinzo to his back and claim the mount position.

8

The moment I land in the mount, I posture up, wrap my left hand around Chinzo's throat, and prepare to unleash a ground and pound assault.

BUTTERFLY GUARD SWEEP

In the sequence below I demonstrate my preferred method for obtaining control of my opponent in the butterfly guard position, as well as a basic but highly effective sweep. I was taught this move back when I was a white belt in Brazilian jiu-jitsu, and for a long time it was the only sweep I utilized. Even now as a black belt, I find it to be the most effective technique in my butterfly guard arsenal. When executed properly, it works on just about anyone, regardless of skill level or body type. Although I utilize the sweep in this scenario to transition into side control, it is important to note that it can also be utilized to transition into the mount. However, when you transition to mount it is very important to immediately hook your legs underneath your opponent's legs. If you don't quickly secure the position, your opponent can use the momentum of the sweep to his advantage by rolling you over to your back. Personally, I feel transitioning to side control is the better option because it offers more stable control. But as with most techniques that offer multiple options, deciding which route to take depends on personal choice.

I've secured the butterfly guard position. Notice my positioning. I've gripped my opponent's left triceps with my right hand, secured a deep left underhook, hooked my left foot to the inside of his right leg, and coiled my right leg underneath my left leg. To prevent him from flattening me to the mat, I've positioned my head underneath his head. From here, I can immediately get my offense going with a sweep.

I pull Chinzo's upper body forward and begin falling toward my right side. There are several things here worth noting. For starters, I keep his left arm trapped underneath my right arm as I fall, which prevents him from posting his left hand on the mat and defending the sweep. Secondly, I fall to my side as opposed to falling straight to my back. If I attempt the latter, my opponent will reestablish his base and most likely block the sweep. Thirdly, I pull my opponent's weight onto his knees to shatter his base, making the sweep easy to pull off. If you fail to accomplish this task, your opponent will most likely maintain his base and block the sweep.

3

Having shattered Chinzo's base with my previous actions, I fall to my right shoulder and elevate his right leg off the mat using my left foot.

4

Continuing to roll over my right shoulder and drive my left foot into his right leg, I sweep Chinzo to his back.

5

As Chinzo's back hits the mat, I post up on my right foot and begin rotating my hips. It's important to note how I keep my left underhook tight and maintain control of his left arm. By keeping my upper body glued to his, I pin his shoulders to the mat and hinder his ability to scramble.

Keeping Chinzo's shoulders pinned to the mat and continuing to rotate my hips in a clockwise direction, I slide my left leg underneath my right leg. Notice that as I do this, I pull his left shoulder slightly off the mat. This will allow me to position my left knee underneath his left shoulder as I establish the side control position.

To secure side control, I slide my left leg underneath Chinzo's left shoulder and then shift my weight over his torso.

HALF GUARD SWEEP

When you have an opponent in the half guard, one of the best ways to get your offensive going is to turn onto your side and establish an underhook. For example, if you have your opponent's right leg trapped between your legs, sitting up to your right side and securing a left underhook is a great way to nullify his attacks and create openings for offensive techniques. However, many fighters will hinder you from reaching this position by posturing up. While in a jiu-jitsu match this poses little threat, it can be a dangerous situation in MMA because your opponent can begin throwing downward strikes. If you should find yourself in this scenario, transitioning into the sweep demonstrated below is an excellent way to avoid taking serious damage. Although the technique is a bit more advanced than some of the other moves that I've shown, it is an invaluable tool to have in your arsenal.

Chinzo is postured up in my half guard. To maintain separation and prevent him from landing punches with his right arm, I place my left foot on his right hip and position my left knee in front of his face. To keep him from landing punches with his left arm, I place my left hand on his left shoulder and position my right arm to the inside of his left arm.

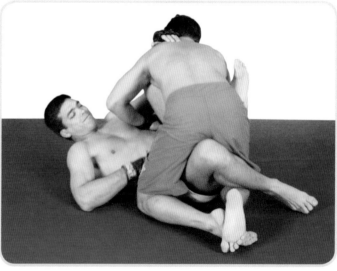

To disrupt Chinzo's base, I roll to my left shoulder, pull down on his left shoulder with my left hand, draw my left knee to my chest, and reach my right hand to the inside of his left leg.

3

To counter my previous actions, Chinzo climbs up to his right foot and plants his right hand on the mat. Note, in order for this sweep to work you have to force your opponent into the standing position. This can be accomplished by rocking his upper body forward and using your right underhook to pull his left leg toward your head.

4

Still trying to reestablish his base, Chinzo plants his left hand on the mat and slides his left foot to the right side of my head. The instant he lands in this position, I hook my right arm around his left leg, plant my left foot on the mat, and place my right foot on the back of his right calf.

5

Having rocked Chinzo's body over me, I trap his left leg by wrapping my right hand behind my head. At the same time, I drive my left foot off the mat to turn my body, roll toward my right shoulder, and push on his left hip using my left hand. With my right foot serving as a barrier to prevent him from counterstepping and reestablishing his balance, he begins plummeting toward his back.

6

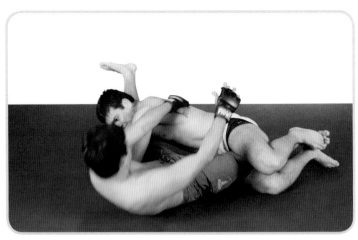

As Chinzo falls to his back, I continue in the direction of my roll, post up onto my right elbow, and begin working for top control.

7

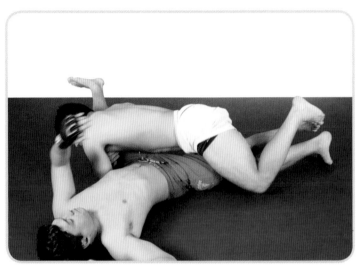

Still rotating my body in a clockwise direction, I plant my left elbow next to Chinzo's left hip and drop my left knee over his right leg.

8

Keeping my right underhook intact, I pull Chinzo's right leg into my chest, slide my left knee underneath my right leg, and drop my weight over his torso. With his legs separated and his back planted to the mat, I will unhook my right leg from around his leg and secure the side control position.

PART SEVEN
ESCAPES

In this section I demonstrate several escapes that can be utilized when your opponent obtains a dominant position, including side control, mount, and back control. In addition to this, I've also included several submission escapes should you find yourself caught in a triangle choke or guillotine choke while in your opponent's guard. With all of the techniques in this section, whether you are defending against a submission or escaping a dominant position, the key to success is implementing your escape the instant your opponent obtains his dominant control or lock. For example, if he manages to pass your guard and transition into side control, you want to immediately work for an underhook and escape to his back. If you delay, you give him a chance to drop his weight over your chest and establish the position, making your escape much harder to execute. If your opponent manages to slap on a triangle choke while you are in his guard, your best chance of surviving is to immediately posture up.

While it is better to never end up in compromising positions, even the best fighters get caught. To avoid getting finished, you must drill the escapes presented in this section until the movements become instinctual. If you panic or tense up in these crisis moments, you will not only burn precious energy, but you will also give your opponent the time and energy he needs to finish the job and put you away.

SIDE CONTROL UNDERHOOK ESCAPE

In the sequence below I demonstrate an effective escape from the bottom side control position. The first step is to position your far arm in front of your opponent's face and then drive his head away from your body. If your opponent resists this pressure, elevating your hips while forcing his head away will often do the trick. The goal is to create space between your bodies, allowing you to secure an underhook with your far arm. Once accomplished, you can use the escape below to transition to your opponent's back or work back up to your feet.

Technical Note: It is important to note that this technique must be done explosively. The instant you secure the underhook and create space, transition up to your knees. If you hesitate, your opponent will wrap his right arm around the back of your left arm, and then cinch down on your underhook with a tight overhook. Although you are still better off than when you didn't have an underhook, your opponent's hold makes it extremely difficult to get up to your knees and escape your head out from underneath his body. In most cases, you will get dragged back to the mat. To prevent such an outcome, explode straight up to your knees the moment you create space with the underhook.

1

I'm stuck underneath Chinzo in the bottom side control position. To set up my escape, I position my left arm in front of his face. Once accomplished, I can use my left arm to create space so that I can escape the position. A lot of fighters make the mistake of wrapping their left arm around their opponent's head. Not only does this strip you of your defensive options, but it also makes you vulnerable to several attacks.

2

To create separation, I extend my left arm upward into Chinzo's face.

3

Capitalizing on the space created with my previous actions, I pummel my left hand to the inside of Chinzo's right arm.

4

I secure a deep left underhook by driving my left arm upward into Chinzo's right armpit. At the same time, I begin rolling toward my right shoulder.

5

As I roll over my right shoulder, I drive my left arm upward into Chinzo's right armpit and rock his upper body over my head.

Machida Karate-Do: Mixed Martial Arts Techniques

6

Having created space with my previous actions, I wrap my left arm over Chinzo's back and start rolling up to my knees.

7

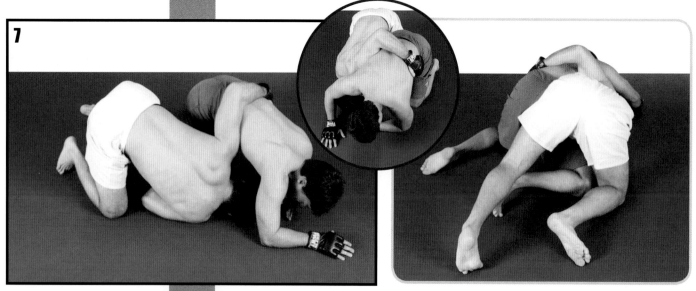

Without hesitation, I climb up to my knees and begin sliding my head out from underneath his body. Notice how I hook my left hand around Chinzo's left side. This not only keeps his body close, which prevents him from scrambling, but it also helps me escape my head.

8

I pull my head out from underneath Chinzo's body. From here, I can throw punches, work to secure control of his back, or stand up to disengage.

HIP ESCAPE FROM MOUNT

In this sequence I demonstrate an effective way to escape the mount. Although it doesn't land you in a dominant position, it puts you in half guard with an underhook, which allows you to immediately get your offensive going. To increase your chances of securing a dominant position, transition into a half guard sweep the instant you arrive in the position. In other words, combine your mount escape and your half guard sweep into one fluid movement. If you hesitate when you establish half guard, your opponent will most likely reestablish his base and begin defending your half guard attacks.

I'm stuck on the bottom mount position.

Before Chinzo can get his offense going, I jam my left elbow to the inside of his right knee, turn onto my left side, drive my right foot off the mat, and slide my hips back. Notice how this action rocks his body forward.

Having rocked Chinzo's upper body forward, I extend my left arm into his right leg and then capitalize on the space created by sliding my left leg underneath his right leg. At the same time, I elevate my right knee and bring my right foot over his right leg.

To trap Chinzo in my half guard, I hook my right foot over of his right leg, secure a left underhook, and then begin rolling toward my right shoulder.

Using my left underhook, I shuck Chinzo's body toward my right side as I roll over my right shoulder. Now on my side with a dominant underhook, I will immediately initiate an attack.

BACK ESCAPE

In the sequence below I demonstrate a technique that not only allows you to escape the rear naked choke when your opponent obtains control of your back, but also transition into the top side control position. It is important to note that your first line of business when your opponent takes your back should always be defense. If your opponent is an experienced grappler, it will only take him a fraction of a second to apply the rear naked choke, so you must immediately focus on protecting your neck. If you look at the photos below, you'll notice that my opponent has his right arm wrapped around my neck. To prevent him from choking me unconscious, I use both of my hands to pull his choking arm downward. Once his forearm is positioned below my neck, I tuck my chin to my chest to close off his access to my throat. No longer in immediate danger of being choked, I immediately begin working on my escape by prying his left leg off the top of my legs. Having regained some mobility, I slide off his body, turn into him, and then establish the side control position. The key to being successful with this technique is focusing on defense first. If you get hasty with your escape, your opponent will lock in the choke, giving you no choice but to tap in submission.

Chinzo has secured control of my back and is working for the rear naked choke. To protect my neck, I grab his right arm with both of my hands and tuck my chin to my chest.

Still using my right hand to defend against the choke, I reach my left hand down to the inside of his left leg and grab the back of his left heel.

3

I rip Chinzo's left foot off of my left leg.

4

Having cleared Chinzo's hook from my left leg, I step my left foot over his leg and begin falling toward my left side.

5

I plant my left foot on the mat to the outside of Chinzo's left leg. At the same time, I slide my body toward my left and escape my hips from between his legs. Notice how I continue to pull down on his right arm with my right hand to loosen his grip on my neck.

6

With my hips free and my back to the mat, I begin turning into Chinzo to secure top control.

7

Turning my body in a clockwise direction, I slide my right leg underneath my left leg and climb up to my knees. To prevent my opponent from turning into me, I hook my left arm to the inside of his right leg.

8

To secure side control, I wrap my left arm around Chinzo's right hip, slide my left knee up to his left hip, and drive my weight forward.

SUBMISSION DEFENSE

POSTURE-UP TRIANGLE ESCAPE

When you are in your opponent's guard and he manages to trap your head and arm between his legs and apply the triangle choke, your best chance of surviving the submission is to immediately posture up. This prevents him from tightening the choke by pulling his foot into the crook of his knee and moving your trapped arm across your body. Once postured, it becomes very easy to break his lock and free your trapped arm, as demonstrated below. However, if your opponent should manage to break your posture, your best option for survival is to employ the technique demonstrated in the next sequence.

Chinzo has managed to trap my head and right arm between his legs and is working to finish me with a triangle choke.

Before Chinzo can pull my head down to lock in the submission, I posture up and look to the ceiling. This action forces his legs apart and will allow me to escape the submission. Remember, you have to be explosive with this step. The instant he traps your head and arm, immediately posture up.

Having broken Chinzo's lock, I grab his right knee with my left hand.

I pull Chinzo's right leg off my left shoulder.

I free my left arm and prepare to unleash a ground and pound assault.

STEP-OVER TRIANGLE ESCAPE

In the previous sequence I demonstrated how to escape the triangle choke by pushing off your opponent's chest and posturing up. Although this is the preferred method of escape, it's not always possible. If your opponent manages to tighten the choke by pulling his foot down into the crook of his knee and moving your trapped arm across your neck, posturing is no longer possible. In this dire situation, immediately wrap your leg over the top of your opponent's body to prevent him from sitting up into you and finishing the lock. Next, lay backward to break his locked legs apart. The escape doesn't land you in the best position, but it is better than getting put to sleep. The key to success with this technique is immediately reacting to your opponent's submission. If you hesitate, chances are you will be waking up with a referee hovering over top of you.

Chinzo has managed to trap my head and right arm between his legs and is working to finish me with a triangle choke. Notice how he has broken my posture by hooking his right foot in the crook of his left leg, as well as pulled my right arm across my neck. To prevent him from pulling my head down and finishing the choke, I will immediately throw my leg over his body and flatten my back to the mat.

Driving my weight forward, I post up on my right foot.

Still driving my weight forward, I come up onto both feet.

4

Posting up on my left leg, I throw my right leg over Chinzo's left arm and head.

5

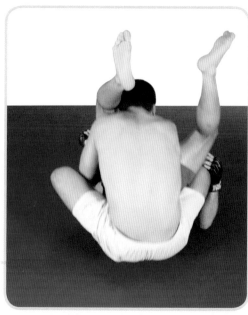

To break Chinzo's lock on my head, I wrap my right leg over his body and sit my butt to the mat.

6

Rolling to my back, I grip my hands together and throw my left foot over my right foot. This prevents Chinzo from sitting up and securing the mount as I flatten my back to the mat. From here, I will scramble and work to improve my position.

GUILLOTINE ESCAPE

There are two common mistakes many fighters make when they get caught in a guillotine choke while in their opponent's guard. First, they attempt to escape the submission by punching their opponent in the face. While this might seem like a good tactic, the majority of the time it gives your opponent the time he needs to lock the choke tight. The second mistake many fighters make is to try and resist the choke by pulling their heads back, which often only cinches the choke tighter. To escape the dangerous submission, the first step is to protect your neck. If you look at the photos below, you'll notice that I accomplish this by grabbing my opponents choking arm and pulling it away from my neck. No longer in immediate danger, I drive all of my weight forward. This stacks my opponent's body and strips him of the leverage he needs to finish the choke. Once accomplished, it becomes quite easy to rip his arm off of my head and resume my offense.

Chinzo has managed to catch me in a guillotine choke. I immediately defend by grabbing his right hand with my left hand.

Driving my weight forward, I wrap my right arm around the back of Chinzo's head and climb up to both feet. It's important to note that I'm distributing all my weight through my right shoulder.

3

Having stripped Chinzo of his leverage, I pull his right hand away from my neck using my left hand.

4

I pull my head out from underneath Chinzo's right arm.

5

I sit back and regain my posture.

Lyoto Machida 4 DVD Box Set

DVD 1
Movement and Fundamental Strikes

DVD 2
Striking Attacks and Takedowns

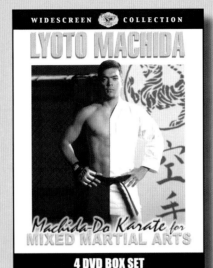

DVD 3
Intercepting Attacks, Takedown Defense, and The Clinch

DVD 4
The Ground Game

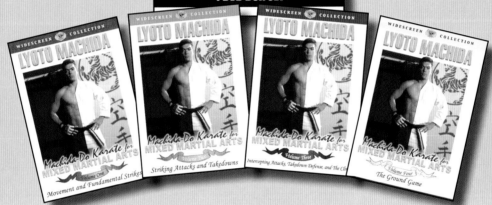

INSTRUCTIONAL DVDs BY ANTONIO RODRIGO NOGUEIRA

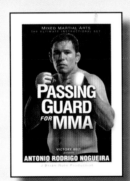
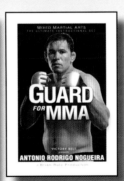
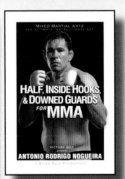

INSTRUCTIONAL DVDs BY ANDERSON SILVA

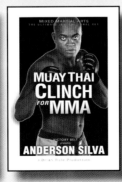
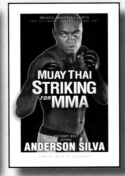
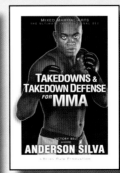
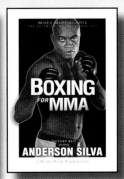

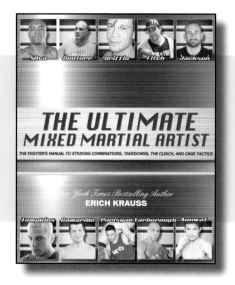

THE ULTIMATE MIXED MARTIAL ARTIST
THE FIGHTER'S MANUAL TO STRIKING COMBINATIONS, TAKEDOWNS, THE CLINCH, AND CAGE TACTICS

ANDERSON SILVA / RANDY COUTURE
FORREST GRIFFIN / JON FITCH / GREG JACKSON
SHAWN THOMPKINS / DAVE CAMARILLO
KARO PARISYAN / SHAWN YARBOROUGH / ANUWAT

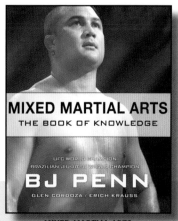

**MIXED MARTIAL ARTS:
THE BOOK OF KNOWLEDGE
BJ PENN**

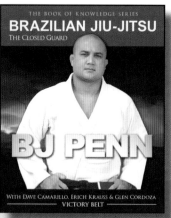

**BRAZILIAN JIU-JITSU:
THE CLOSED GUARD
BJ PENN**

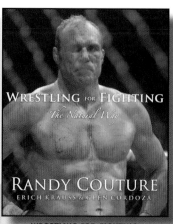

**WRESTLING FOR FIGHTING:
THE NATURAL WAY
RANDY COUTURE**

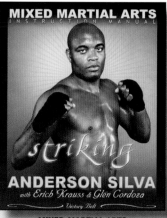

**MIXED MARTIAL ARTS
INSTRUCTION MANUAL: STRIKING
ANDERSON SILVA**

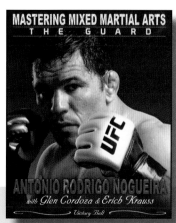

**MASTERING MIXED MARTIAL ARTS:
THE GUARD
ANTONIO NOGUEIRA**

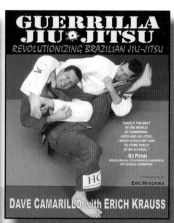

**GUERRILLA JIU-JITSU:
REVOLUTIONIZING BRAZILIAN JIU-JITSU
DAVE CAMARILLO**

**MASTERING THE RUBBER GUARD:
JIU-JITSU FOR MMA COMPETITION
EDDIE BRAVO**

**MASTERING THE TWISTER:
JIU-JITSU FOR MMA COMPETITION
EDDIE BRAVO**

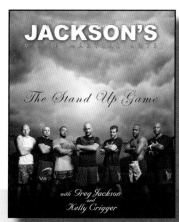

**JACKSON'S MIXED MARTIAL ARTS
THE STAND-UP GAME
GREG JACKSON**

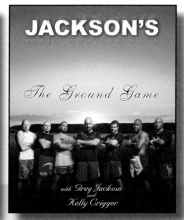

**JACKSON'S MIXED MARTIAL ARTS
THE GROUND GAME
GREG JACKSON**

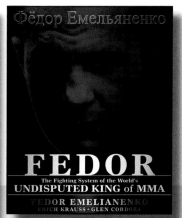

**FEDOR: THE FIGHTING SYSTEM OF THE
UNDISPUTED KING OF MMA
FEDOR EMELIANENKO**

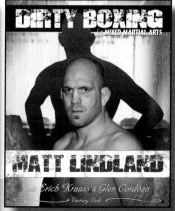

**DIRTY BOXING
FOR MIXED MARTIAL ARTS
MATT LINDLAND**

**THE X-GUARD
GI & NO GI JIU-JITSU
MARCELO GARCIA**

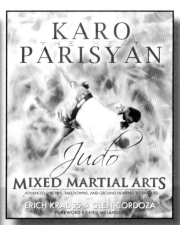

**JUDO FOR MMA: ADVANCED THROWS,
TAKEDOWNS, AND GROUND FIGHTING
KARO PARISYAN**

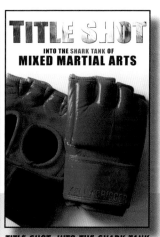

**TITLE SHOT: INTO THE SHARK TANK
OF MIXED MARTIAL ARTS
KELLY CRIGGER**

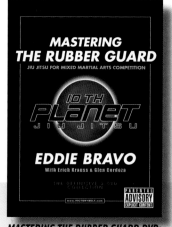

**MASTERING THE RUBBER GUARD DVD:
JIU-JITSU FOR MMA COMPETITION
EDDIE BRAVO**

LYOTO "THE DRAGON" MACHIDA has been involved in martial arts since birth. The son of Japanese Shotokan karate master Yoshizo Machida, Lyoto holds a black belt in Machida Karate-Do and Brazilian Jiu-Jitsu. Undefeated in mixed martial arts competition and the current UFC light heavyweight champion, he is considered by many publications to be the number one light heavyweight in the world. He currently lives and trains at his family's dojo in Belem, Brazil.

CHINZO MACHIDA, older brother of Lyoto Machida, is a Shotokan karate black belt and the Japan Karate Association Vice Champion (Sydney, Australia 2006). In addition to helping Lyoto train for his fights, he also teaches classes at their family dojo in Belem, Brazil.

GLEN CORDOZA, is a professional Muay Thai kickboxer and mixed martial artist. Author of twelve books on the martial arts, Cordoza has worked with some of the world's top athletes, including Randy Couture, BJ Penn, Fedor Emelianenko, Anderson Silva, Matt Lindland, and Antonio Nogueira. He is currently living and training out of Las Vegas, Nevada.